Janice VanCleave's

A+
PROJECTS IN
EARTH
SCIENCE
Winning Experiments for
Science Fairs and Extra Credit

SCHOLASTIC INC.

New York   Toronto   London   Auckland   Sydney
Mexico City   New Delhi   Hong Kong

ISBN 0-439-24422-6

The original publisher and the author have made every reasonable effort to ensure
that the experiments and activities in this book are safe when conducted as instructed
but assume no responsibility for any damage caused or sustained while performing
the experiments or activities in the book. Parents, guardians, and/or teachers should
supervise young readers who undertake the experiments and activities in this book.

12 11 10 9 8 7 6 5 4 3 2 1   1 2 3 4 5 6/0

Printed in the U.S.A.   23

First Scholastic printing, February 2001

Dedication

This book is dedicated
to
my husband, Wade, for his love and constant support;
to
my children and grandchildren, Tina and Mike Ryer;
Ginger, Russell, Kimberly, Jennifer, David
and Davin VanCleave; and Ginger, Calvin,
Lauren, and Lacey Russell;
to
friends Jim, Stella, Rachel Anne, Jared Lee, and
Sara Elizabeth Cathey; Whitney Cooper; Sue and
Fred Dunham; Sara, Rachel, James, and Mary Catherine
Blalock; Adam and Lauren Nicole Himsel; David,
Garrett, and Amber Kaiser; Laura, Jim, and Adelaide
Roberts; Sarah, Jared, Jacob, and Jordan Sacchieri;
Weston Ray; and Patrick Walker;
to
my editor, Kate Bradford; my production editors,
Benjamin Hamilton, Joanne Palmer,
and Jude Patterson.

Contents

Introduction

Science is a search for answers to all kinds of interesting questions about our world. Science projects make excellent tools for you to use as you look for the answers to specific problems. This book will give you guidance and provide A+ project ideas. An A+ idea is not a guarantee that you will receive an A+ on your project. You must do your part by planning experiments, finding and recording information related to a problem, and organizing the data to find the answer.

Sharing your findings by presenting your project at science fairs will be a rewarding experience if you have properly prepared the exhibit. Trying to assemble a project overnight usually results in frustration, and you cheat yourself out of the fun of being a science detective. Solving a scientific mystery, like solving a detective mystery, requires that you plan well and carefully collect facts.

Start your project with curiosity and a desire to learn something new. Then, proceed with purpose and a determination to solve the problem. It is likely that your scientific quest will end with some interesting answers.

Select a Topic

The 30 topics in this book suggest many possible problems to solve. Each topic has one "cookbook" experiment—follow the recipe, and the result is guaranteed. Read all of these easy experiments before choosing the topic you like best and want to know more about. Regardless of the problem you choose to solve, your discoveries will make you more knowledgeable about earth science.

Each of the 30 sample projects begins with a brief summary of topics to be studied and objectives to be determined. Information relevant to the project is also included in the opening summary. Terms are defined when first used in the project discussion, but definitions are not repeated throughout the text. Check the Glossary or Index to find explanations about any terms that are unfamiliar to you.

Try New Approaches

Following each of the 30 introductory experiments is a section titled "Try New Approaches" that provides additional questions about the problem presented. By making small changes to some part of the sample experiment, you achieve new results. Think about why these new results might have happened.

Design Your Own Experiment

In each chapter, the section titled "Design Your Own Experiment" allows you to create experiments to solve questions related to the sample experiment. Your own experiment should follow the sample experiment's format and include a single purpose or statement; a list of necessary materials; a detailed step-by-step procedure; written results with diagrams, graphs, and charts, if they seem helpful; and a conclusion explaining why you got the results you did and answering the question you posed to yourself. To clarify your answer, include any information you found through research. When you design your own experiment, make sure to get adult approval if supplies or procedures other than those given in this book are used.

Get the Facts

Read about your topic in many books and magazines. You are more likely to have a successful project if you are well informed about the topic. For each topic in this book, the section titled "Get the Facts" provides some tips to guide you to specific sources of information. Keep a journal to record all the information you find from each source, including the author's name, the title of the book or article, the page numbers, the publisher's name, the city of publication, and the year of publication.

Keep a Journal

Purchase a bound notebook to serve as your journal. Write in it everything relating to the project. It should contain your original ideas as well as ideas you get from books or from people like teachers and scientists. It should also include descriptions of your experiments as well as diagrams, photographs, and written observations of all your results.

Every entry should be as neat as possible and dated. A neat, orderly journal provides a complete and accurate record of your project from start to finish and can be used to write your project report. It is also proof of the time you spent sleuthing out the answers to the scientific mystery you undertook to solve, and you will want to display the journal with your completed project.

Use the Scientific Method

Each project idea in this book will provide foundation material to guide you in planning what could be a prize-winning project. With your topic in mind and some background information, you are ready to demonstrate a scientific principle or to solve a scientific problem via the **scientific method**. This method of scientifically finding answers involves the following steps: research, purpose, hypothesis, experimentation, and conclusion.

Research: The process of collecting information about the topic being studied. It is listed as a first step because some research must be done first to formulate the purpose and hypothesis and then to explain experimental results.

Purpose: A statement that expresses the problem or question for which you are seeking resolution. You must have some knowledge about a topic before you can formulate a question that can lead to problem-solving experimentation. Thus, some research is necessary before you state a purpose, and you can find much of the information about each topic in this book.

Hypothesis: A guess about the answer to the problem based on prior knowledge and on research you have done before beginning the project. It is most important to write down your hypothesis before beginning the project and not to change it even if experimentation proves you wrong.

Experimentation: The process of testing your hypothesis. Safety is of utmost importance. The projects in this book are designed to encourage you to learn more about an earth science phenomenon by altering a known procedure, but you should explore untested procedures only with adult supervision.

Conclusion: A summary of the experimental results and a statement that addresses how the results relate to the purpose of the experiment. Reasons for experimental results that are contrary to the hypothesis are included.

Assemble the Display

Keep in mind that while your display represents all that you have done, it must tell the story of the project in such a way that it

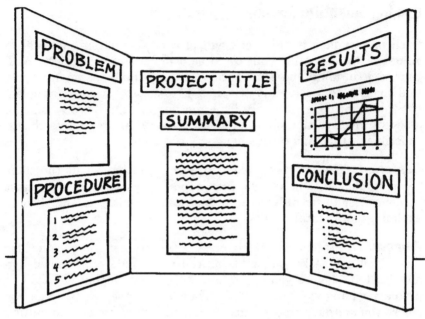

Figure I.1

attracts and holds the viewer's interest. So keep it simple. Try not to cram all your information into one place. To conserve space on the display and still exhibit all your work, keep some of the charts, graphs, pictures, and other materials in your journal instead of on the display board itself.

The actual size and shape of displays vary according to local science fair official rules, so remember to check them out for your particular fair. Most exhibits are allowed to be 48 inches (122 cm) wide, 30 inches (76 cm) deep, and 108 inches (274 cm) high. Your display may be smaller than these maximum measurements. A three-sided backboard (see Figure I.1) is usually the best way to display your work. Wooden panels can be hinged together, or you can use sturdy cardboard pieces taped together to form a very inexpensive, but presentable, exhibit.

A good title of about eight words or less should be placed at the top of the center panel. The title should capture the theme of the project but not be the same as the problem statement. For example, suppose the problem under question is, What is the best type of soil for plant growth? An effective title might be "Effects of Soil Porosity and Permeability on Plant Growth." The title and other headings should be neat and also large enough to be readable from a distance of about 3 feet (1 m). You can glue letters onto the backboard (buy precut letters or cut some out of construction paper), or use a computer to create them for all the titles. A short summary paragraph of about 100 words to explain the scientific principles involved is useful and can be printed under the title. Someone who has no knowledge of the topic should be able to easily understand the basic idea of the project just by reading the summary.

There are no set rules about the position of the information on the display. However, it all needs to be well organized, with the title and summary paragraph as the focal point at the top of the center panel and the remaining material placed neatly from left to right under specific headings. The headings you display will depend on how you wish to organize the information. Separate headings of "Problem," "Procedure," "Results," and "Conclusion" may be used.

Discuss the Project

The judges give points for how clearly you are able to discuss the project and explain its purpose, procedure, results, and conclusion. While the display should be organized so that it explains everything, your ability to discuss your project and answer the questions of the judges convinces them that you did the work and understand what you have done. Practice a speech in front of friends, and invite them to ask you questions. If you do not know the answer to a question, never guess or make up an answer or just say, "I do not know." Instead, say that you did not discover that answer during your research, and then offer other information that you found of interest about the project. Be proud of the project, and approach the judges with enthusiasm about your work.

Mapping the Earth

1 | Maps and Globes: Terrestrial Guides

A map is a representation of all or part of a region of the Earth's surface. Maps can be spherical like the Earth or flat. They all have criss-crossing lines that are used to indicate the coordinates of any specific location. These reference lines are called meridians (or lines of longitude) and parallels (or lines of latitude).

In this project, you will study and model the meridians and parallels. You will learn a technique for measuring latitude and determine the latitude where you live. Planar projection, a method of preparing flat maps, will also be demonstrated.

Getting Started

Purpose: To model meridians (lines of longitude) on a globe.

Materials

lemon-size ball of   dental floss
   modeling clay
pencil

Procedure

1. Shape the clay into a sphere.
2. Use the pencil to draw a circle around the center of the clay sphere.
3. Draw a second circle perpendicular to the first one.
4. Hold the sphere so the lines cross at its top and bottom ends.
5. Observe the position of the lines and the distance between them at (1) the ends of the sphere where the lines cross, and (2) the center of the sphere, midway between the ends.
6. Wrap the ends of the dental floss around your index fingers, then use your thumbs to press the floss into one of the circles. Press the floss through the clay sphere, cutting the sphere in half (see Figure 1.1).

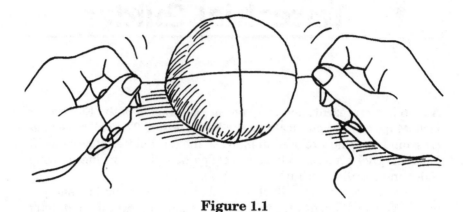

Figure 1.1

Results

The lines you drew with the pencil are not parallel. They approach and cross each other at opposite ends of the sphere and are farthest apart around the center of the sphere. Cutting through the clay creates a plane that passes through the center of the sphere.

Why?

The circles around the clay sphere are called **great circles** (circles on a sphere, with the center of the circle and the center of the sphere being the same). A **meridian** is defined as a great circle, or half of a great circle passing through the Earth's **North** and **South Poles** (northernmost and southernmost points on the Earth). In this book, meridian will refer to half of a great circle. Thus, the clay model has four meridians from pole to pole. While there is no limit to the number of meridians that may be on a globe, a common number of meridians is 24.

Meridians are also called **lines of longitude** because they measure longitude. **Longitude** is the distance in degrees east and west of the meridian running through Greenwich, England, called the **prime meridian**. The prime meridian is located at 0° longitude. Longitudes 0° and 180° divide a globe into the Eastern and Western Hemispheres, as demonstrated by cutting the clay model in half. (The word **hemisphere** means half a sphere.) In the **Eastern Hemisphere** the longitudes are 0° to 180° and are labeled with an E, such as 90° E. The **Western Hemisphere** longitudes making up the other half of the sphere also start at 0° and end at 180°; they are labeled with a W, such as 90° W. Note that 90° E and 90° W are on opposite sides of the sphere from each other and that 0° E and 0° W are the same meridian, as are 180° E and 180° W.

The lines on the clay sphere, like the meridians on a globe, are not parallel. The distance between the meridians is greatest at the middle of the globe and decreases toward the poles (ends). One degree (1°) of longitude is about 69 miles (110 km) wide at the equator and gradually narrows to 0 miles (0 km) wide at the North and South Poles.

Try New Approaches

Circles around a globe that run parallel to each other and perpendicular to the meridians are called **parallels**. The parallel that runs around the center of the globe, equidistant to the Poles and the only one that is a great circle, is called the **equator**. Parallels are also called **lines of latitude** because they measure latitude. **Latitude** is the distance in degrees north or south of the equator, which is located at 0° latitude. The equator divides the globe into the **Northern** and **Southern Hemispheres**. The latitudes in each hemisphere range from 0° to 90°. Latitudes are labeled N in the Northern Hemisphere and S in the Southern Hemisphere.

Prepare a model showing lines of longitude and lines of latitude. Repeat steps 1 through 4 from the original experiment, then draw a circle around the middle of the sphere, halfway between the poles and perpendicular to the lines of longitude. This line represents the equator. Draw two more circles on either side of the equator, parallel to it, each centered between the equator and a pole. These two circles represent lines of latitude at 45° north and south of the equator.

Design Your Own Experiment

1. In the Northern Hemisphere, you can determine your latitude by measuring the height of the North Star (Polaris) above the horizon. To do this, you can use an **astrolabe**, an instrument used to measure the altitude of a **celestial body** (a natural object in the sky, such as a star, sun, moon, or planet). Make an astrolabe by tying one end of a 12-inch (30-cm) string through the center hole in the base of a protractor. Attach the free end of the string to a washer. Tape a drinking straw along the straight edge of the protractor. Without covering the lines, place pieces of masking tape on the protractor and write 0 to 90 on the pieces of tape, as shown in Figure 1.2.

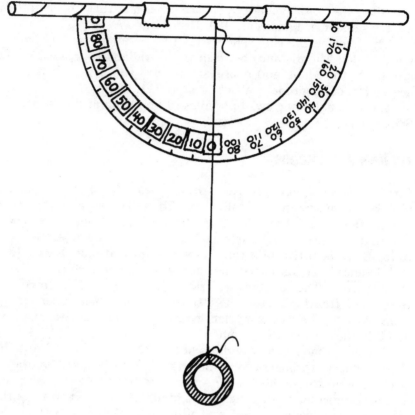

Figure 1.2

Stand outdoors on a dark, clear night and find the North Star by lining up the two outermost stars in the bowl of the Big Dipper. The North Star, a relatively faint star, is directly ahead of these two stars. Close one eye and use the other eye to look through the viewing end of the straw. Sight the North Star through the straw. Ask a helper to use an astronomer's flashlight (see Appendix 3) to read the angle where the string crosses the protractor. This angle is equal to the latitude of the area where you are.

2. While globes most accurately represent the Earth, they are not 100% accurate. Flat maps are less accurate than globes, but flat maps are less expensive and easier to carry around. All methods

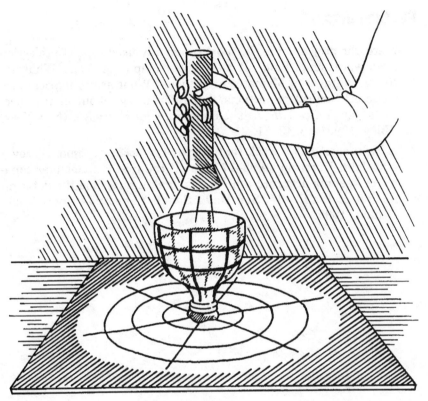

Figure 1.3

of making a flat map of the curved Earth involve some inaccuracies. Map projection is one method of producing a flat map. A **planar projection** is a circular map that shows only one hemisphere of the Earth.

Demonstrate how to make a planar projection by cutting off the top 5 inches (12.5 cm) of a 2-liter plastic soda bottle. Use the top section of the bottle to model a hemisphere. Using a rubber band as a guide, draw three or four latitude lines around the outside of the bottle with a black permanent marker. Draw six or eight longitude lines. In the center of a piece of white poster board, stand the bottle in a walnut-size piece of clay so that the cut end of the bottle points upward. In a darkened room, hold a flashlight above the center of the model (see Figure 1.3). Ask a helper to trace the projection on the poster board.

Get the Facts

1. Mercator projection is the most commonly used type of projection for a world map. Find out more about map projections. What are the advantages of Mercator projections? What are cylindrical projections? Conical projections? For information about map projections, see *Janice VanCleave's Geography for Every Kid* (New York: Wiley, 1993), pp. 43–51.

2. A *chronometer* is a clock that keeps very accurate time. Discover how John Harrison (1693–1776) built the first chronometer capable of keeping accurate time at sea, making possible the determination of longitude. See Dava Sobel, *Longitude* (New York: Walker, 1995).

Topography: Highs and Lows of the Earth's Surface

2

The Earth's surface has features with different elevations, such as mountains, valleys, and lakes, called topography. Three-dimensional (3-D) models, topographic maps, and profile diagrams can be used to show the elevation of surface features.

In this project, you will show how topographic maps use contour lines to indicate the elevation of a land area. You will determine the effect that changes in elevation have on the distance between the map's contour lines. You will use marks called hachures to indicate depressions and craters on your map. You will also measure the elevation of a gently sloping hill, draw a profile map of the hill, and make a 3-D model of the profile of the hill.

Getting Started

Purpose: To produce a 3-D model of a mountain.

Materials

apple-size ball of clay

sheet of typing paper

metric ruler

about 30 toothpicks

pen

Procedure

1. Lay aside a grape-size piece of clay. Use the remaining clay to mold a mountain with an uneven landscape. Make depressions in the side and/or a crater (a hollowed-out area at the top of a volcano) in the top.

2. Set the clay mountain in the center of the paper.

3. Insert the zero end of the metric ruler into the grape-size piece of clay, and stand the ruler vertically next to the clay mountain.

4. On one side of the clay mountain, use a toothpick to draw a straight vertical line from the top of the mountain to its base.

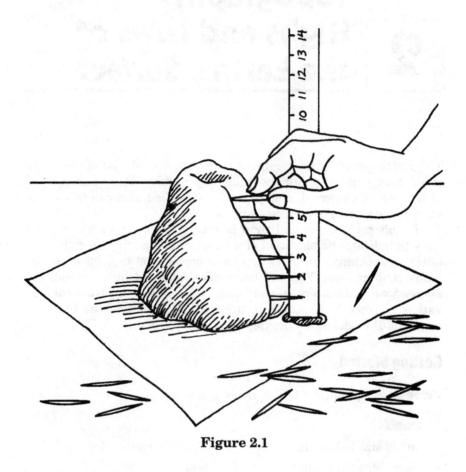

Figure 2.1

5. Align the vertical line drawn on the clay with the edge of the ruler, then mark heights 1 cm apart on the clay mountain: Holding the toothpick horizontally across the 1-cm mark on the ruler, insert the end of the toothpick into the line on the clay. Repeat this procedure at each centimeter mark until you reach the top of the mountain (see Figure 2.1).

6. Turn the mountain one quarter turn and repeat steps 4 and 5. Repeat the procedure two more times so that heights are marked on four sides of the mountain.

Results

A mountain model with different indicated heights is made.

Why?

In this experiment, you made a 3-D model of a mountain. The tooth-picks are placed at different heights to indicate **elevation** (height above sea level).

Try New Approaches

Topography is the description of the size, shape, and elevation of a region of land. A **topographic map** is a flat map that shows the shapes and heights of a land area using **contour lines** (lines that connect points on a map that have the same elevation). The difference in elevation between one contour line and the next is called the **contour interval**. The contour interval on the map in this experiment is 1 cm.

How can a topographic map of the clay mountain be made? Make the map by removing the ruler and following these steps:

1. Use a pen to trace around the base of the mountain. Make a mark on the paper at each vertical line on the clay model.

2. Wrap an 18-inch (45-cm) piece of dental floss around the mountain at the 1-cm height, letting the floss rest on the toothpicks. Cross the ends of the floss, then pull them in opposite directions to cut through the clay model.

3. Lift the top section of the clay straight up, remove the bottom slice without moving the paper, and lower the top section. The lines on the clay should match the marks on the paper. Trace around the base of the clay.

4. Repeat steps 2 and 3 for the remaining heights marked on the clay with toothpicks.

5. Remove the top, final section of the clay mountain from the paper and observe the tracings on the paper.

6. Label the contour lines with the appropriate elevations, as shown in Figure 2.2. Use **hachures** (short lines drawn inside a contour line) to indicate a depression or crater. The free ends of these lines always point downslope.

The closeness of the contour lines indicates the **slope** (the degree of steepness of an inclined surface) of the land. When the lines are far apart, the slope is gentle, but when they are close together, the slope is steep. **Science Fair Hint:** Stack the slices of each clay mountain and display the models along with their topographic maps.

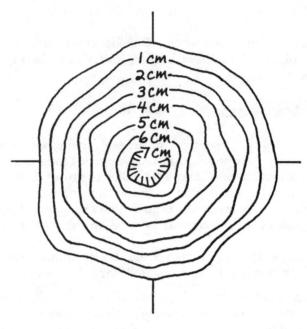

Figure 2.2

Design Your Own Experiment

1a. You can measure the elevation of a small, gently sloping hill by using two rods, such as dowels or plastic pipes, each 2 m long. Using a pen and a meterstick, mark a circle around the center of one rod. Above and below this center mark, use the pen and the meterstick to mark every tenth of a meter, or decimeter (dm). With 0 at the center mark, first number every decimeter above zero as a positive number (1 to 10), then number every decimeter below zero as a negative number (–1 to –10). Tie a string at least 3 m long around the center of the unmarked rod. Stand the rods together so that the string around the unmarked rod is at the same height as the center mark on the marked rod. Secure the string with tape so that it cannot slide up or down the unmarked rod. Tie the free end of the string loosely to a ring, such as a jar ring, that is larger than the diameter of the marked rod. Place the ring over the marked rod. Stand the rods about 3 m apart and adjust the knot around the ring so the string is taut.

To measure a hill, stand on level ground at the base of the hill with your back to the hill. Hold the unmarked rod upright on the

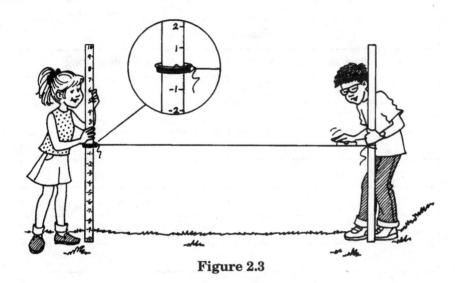

Figure 2.3

ground. Have your helper stand about 3 m away from you, facing you and the hill. Your helper should hold the marked rod upright so that the negative 10-dm mark is touching the ground and the string between the two rods is taut. Level the string by placing a line level (available in hardware stores) on the string near your rod. Instruct your helper to slowly move the ring up or down the marked rod until you can see the bubble in the center of the line level. This indicates that the string is level. Have your helper note the decimeter mark nearest the ring. The mark should be approximately zero. If the mark isn't zero, both you and your helper should very slowly move away from the hill until the ring at the end of the level string is at the zero mark (see Figure 2.3).

The base of the hill is interval 0, and the measurement is 0 dm. Record this measurement in a table similar to Table 2.1. To take the measurement for interval 1, have your helper put his rod in place of yours at the base of the hill. Then move up the hill about 3 m until the string is again taut. Level the string as before, have your helper note the decimeter mark, and record this measurement as interval 1. This and all uphill measurements should be positive numbers. Repeat this procedure, recording each 3-m interval up the hill until you reach the top of the hill. To take downhill measurements, have your helper put his rod in place of yours at the top of the hill. Then move down the hill until the string is again taut. Level the string and record the measurement as before. This and all downhill measurements should be

Table 2.1 Hill	
Interval (3 m)	Measurement (dm)
0	0
1	5
2	10
3	2
4	8
5	-2
6	-10
7	-8
8	-5

negative numbers. Measure each 3-m interval down the hill until the measurement is again approximately zero and your helper has reached the base of the hill.

b. To map the profile (side view) of the hill measured in the previous experiment, follow the procedure described here for the data in Table 2.1 and the graph in Figure 2.4. Each square on the graph paper is equal to 5 dm, and each six squares across represent 30 dm, or 3 m, the measurement interval. The dots labeled 0

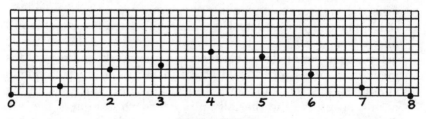

Profile of Hill 1

Figure 2.4

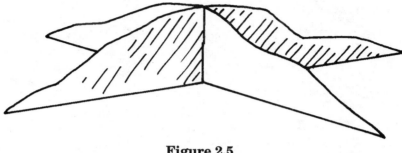

Figure 2.5

to 8 represent the measurements for intervals 0 to 8. Interval 0, the base of the hill, is marked by a dot labeled 0 in the bottom left corner. Each successive dot is placed six squares, or 3 m, to the right of the preceding dot. The dot is placed above the preceding dot depending on the interval measurement. Thus, because the measurement for interval 1 is 5 dm, the dot for interval 1 is placed one square, or 5 dm, above the dot for interval 0, and so on. The downhill or depression measurements are negative numbers and therefore are placed below the preceding dots. Thus, the dot for interval 5 is 2 cm below the dot for interval 4, and so on.

c. Make a 3-D model of the hill by measuring and graphing the hill at a 90° angle to the first path. Cut out the two profiles from the graph paper and use these as patterns to cut the shapes from stiff paper. Make a vertical cut on each profile so they fit together. Cut one profile halfway down from the highest point; cut the other halfway up from the bottom. Fit the profiles together at a 90° angle.

Get the Facts

Cartography is the making or study of maps or charts. Find out more about mapping. What is a relief map? See H. J. de Blij, *The Earth: An Introduction to Its Physical and Human Geography* (New York: Wiley, 1995), pp. 15–26.

The Earth and Space

Rotation:
3 The Spinning of the Earth on Its Axis

The Earth rotates around an imaginary axis. The Poles of the Earth are at the ends of the axis. The North Pole is at the north end, and the South Pole is at the south end.

In this project, you will model a Foucault pendulum to examine the relation between the Earth's rotation and the inertia of free-swinging objects. You will calculate the apparent shift of the path traced by pendulums at different latitudes. You will also model the deflection of fluids due to the Coriolis effect.

Getting Started

Purpose: To model a Foucault pendulum.

Materials

8-inch (20-cm) piece of string

metal washer

pencil

1-quart (1-liter) jar

lazy Susan turntable

masking tape

Procedure

1. Tie one end of the string to the washer.
2. Tie the free end of the string to the center of the pencil.
3. Center the pencil across the mouth of the jar so that the washer is suspended inside the jar.
4. Set the jar on the turntable.
5. Spin the turntable counterclockwise and adjust the position of the jar and/or pencil so that the string hangs straight down as the turntable spins.
6. Stop the turntable and secure the pencil to the jar with tape.
7. Tilt the jar to start the washer moving back and forth in one direction. Set the jar back in place on the turntable.

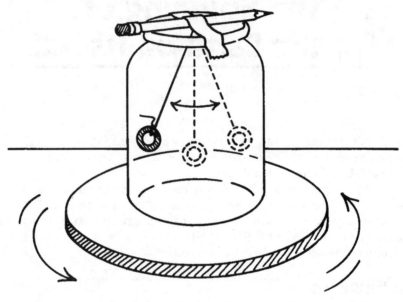

Figure 3.1

8. While the washer is swinging, spin the turntable in a counter-clockwise direction as before (see Figure 3.1).

Results

The washer continues to swing back and forth in the same direction though the jar is turning around. In relationship to the turntable, the swinging washer appears to move in a clockwise direction.

Why?

The turntable represents the Earth **rotating**, which means it is turning about its **axis** (imaginary line that passes through the North and South Poles). As viewed from a position above the North Pole, the Earth rotates in a counterclockwise direction, like the turntable. The washer is a **pendulum** (a suspended object that swings back and forth). A pendulum swings in one direction because of **inertia** (the tendency of an object to remain stationary or to continue moving in a straight line unless acted on by an outside force). The swinging washer did not change direction, but the movement of the turntable made the pendulum seem to move in a clockwise direction, opposite to the rotation of the turntable. A pendulum placed at the North Pole would seem to move in a clockwise direction as seen by an observer on Earth, like the washer in the jar, even though inertia in fact keeps the pendulum swinging in one direction.

A similar experiment was first performed in 1851 by a French physicist, Jean-Bernard-Léon Foucault (1819–1868). Foucault used a 223-foot (67-m) wire to suspend a sphere weighing 62 pounds (28 kg) from the dome of the Panthéon, a public building in Paris. The pendulum was free to move in any direction, but once it was set in motion, inertia kept it swinging in the same direction. A pin at the end of the pendulum made marks in sand on the floor. As time passed, the direction of the marks changed. Because of inertia, the pendulum swung in the same direction. Since the sand rested on the floor of the building, and the building rested on the Earth, the pendulum showed that the Earth itself moves. Thus, Foucault's experiment showed the rotation of the Earth. A pendulum that shows the rotation of the Earth is called a **Foucault pendulum**.

Try New Approaches

As seen from a position above the South Pole, the rotation of the Earth is clockwise. How would the apparent path of a pendulum be affected if the pendulum were placed at the South Pole? Repeat the experiment, rotating the turntable in a clockwise direction.

Design Your Own Experiment

1a. The path traced by a Foucault pendulum appears to shift as the Earth rotates. The amount of the apparent shift of the pendulum's path depends on the latitude of the pendulum's location. At the Poles (latitude 90°), the apparent shift of the pendulum's path is 15° per hour, but at lower latitudes the shift decreases and at the equator (latitude 0°), the apparent shift is 0° per hour—the path doesn't shift at all. The apparent shift (d) in degrees per hour can be calculated for a given latitude using the following equation:

$$d = 15° \sin(\text{latitude})$$

To find sin(latitude), enter the latitude on a scientific calculator and hit the sine function key.

Example:
Foucault's original pendulum was located in Paris, which is at latitude 47° N. Calculate the apparent shift of the pendulum's path in degrees per hour.

$$d = 15° \sin(47)$$
$$= 15°(0.7314)$$
$$= 10.97° \text{ per hour}$$

Use the example to determine the shift of a Foucault pendulum at your latitude.

b. It takes 24 hours for the pendulum to make an apparent 360° shift at either the North or South Pole, but it takes longer at the lower latitudes. The time (t) it takes for the pendulum to make an apparent shift through a complete revolution of 360° at a specific latitude can be calculated by using this equation:

$$t = 360°/d$$

where d is the apparent shift of the pendulum's path in degrees per hour, as calculated in the previous experiment.

Example:
Calculate the time for the path of Foucault's pendulum in Paris to shift 360°.

$$t = 360°/d$$
$$= 360°/10.97° \text{ per hour}$$
$$= 32.82 \text{ hours}$$

Use the equation to determine the time it takes for a pendulum's path to apparently shift 360° at your latitude.

2. The Earth's rotation affects **fluids** (gases or liquids) such as winds and ocean currents that move freely across the Earth by causing them to **deflect** (turn aside from a straight path) and move in curved paths. This deflection of fluids as a result of the Earth's rotation is called the **Coriolis effect**.

Make a model to demonstrate the curved paths of fluids due to the Coriolis effect. Cut an 8-inch (20-cm) circle from a sheet of paper. Use a paper punch to make a hole in the center of the paper circle. Insert a paper brad through the hole in the center of a ruler and the hole in the paper circle. Lay the paper circle on a table with the ruler on top. Use masking tape to tape the ends of the ruler to the table. Position the point of a ballpoint pen at the top of the paper and to one side of the ruler, as shown in Figure 3.2. Draw a line on the paper along the edge of the ruler with a black pen. This straight line shows the path of fluids without the Coriolis effect. Repeat the procedure using the same paper but a red pen. Align the black mark next to the ruler. With your red pen at the top of the paper as before, ask a helper to slowly rotate the paper circle counterclockwise as you draw a line on the paper as before. The curved red line shows the path of fluids with the Coriolis effect. **Science Fair Hint:** Use the drawings as part of a

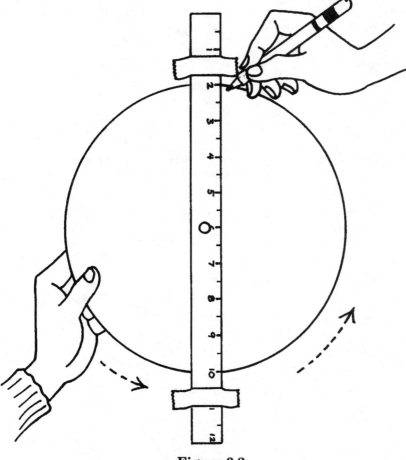

Figure 3.2

project display representing the path of fluids with and without the Coriolis effect.

Get the Facts

The major wind patterns on the Earth are called *prevailing winds.* How does the Earth's rotation affect the direction of these winds? For information, see *Janice VanCleave's Oceans for Every Kid* (New York: Wiley, 1996), pp. 65–75.

4 | Heliocentric: The Earth's Solar System

Our solar system is heliocentric, which means there is a sun in the center and the celestial bodies of the solar system move around the sun. The Earth is one of the nine planets in our solar system.

In this project, you will study the relative position of the Sun in the sky as seen by an observer on Earth. You will map the apparent path of the Sun during the day and at different times of the year. You will also examine the history of the theories of the movement of the celestial bodies in our solar system.

Getting Started

Purpose: To demonstrate the apparent movement of the Sun across the sky using a heliocentric model.

Materials

sheet of typing paper

pencil

2-quart (2-liter) clear glass bowl

gooseneck table lamp

five to six ¾-inch (1.9-cm) round yellow labels

Procedure

1. Place the paper on a table and mark an X in the center of the paper.

2. Turn the bowl upside down on the paper with the X in the center of the bowl.

3. Position the lamp so that the lightbulb is about 12 inches (30 cm) above the tabletop and about 12 inches (30 cm) from the rim of the bowl.

4. On the lamp side of the bowl, hold one of the labels near, but not touching, the bowl.

5. Move the label until its shadow falls on the X mark, then stick it to the bowl.

6. Rotate the bowl slightly in a counterclockwise direction.

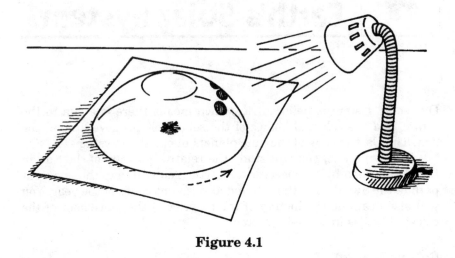

Figure 4.1

7. Repeat steps 4 and 5 twice, using the remaining labels (see Figure
   4.1).

Results

The labels are placed in a line around the bowl with their shadows
falling on the X.

Why?

In this **heliocentric** (sun-centered) model, the lightbulb represents
the Sun. The labels represent the changing apparent position of the
Sun in the sky during the day as seen from the Earth. In this experiment, to an observer on Earth, represented by the X, the Sun appears
to move around the sky at the same altitude. This view of the Sun
would be made at the Earth's Poles during the summer. At this time,
the Sun is above the horizon all day and moves in a very tight spiral
as it rises to a maximum altitude of 23½° on or about December 21,
then slowly starts its descent. (At the Poles, the Sun is above the horizon for half the year and below the horizon for the other half.)
Actually, the Sun is not moving. Instead, the Earth is rotating on its
axis, giving the illusion that the Sun is moving across the sky. Since
the axis of the Earth is tilted in relationship to the Sun, the maximum
height of the Sun in the sky during the day changes as the Earth
revolves (moves in a curved path about an object) around the Sun.
During part of the trip around the Sun, the north axis (North Pole) is
tilted toward the Sun, and during part of the trip, the south axis
(South Pole) is tilted toward the Sun.

The Earth or any celestial body that revolves around another celestial body is called a **satellite**. The curved path that a satellite traces is called an **orbit.**

Try New Approaches

At latitudes between the polar regions, 66½° N and 66½° S, the Sun rises and sets each day. The height of the Sun depends on whether the Earth's axis is tilted toward or away from the Sun. Repeat the experiment twice. First, represent the Earth's axis tilted away from the Sun by raising the bowl on the side facing the lamp. Keep the bowl raised by placing a book under the bowl on that side. Repeat again, raising the bowl on the side away from the lamp to represent the tilt of the axis toward the Sun.

Design Your Own Experiment

1a. Map the apparent path of the Sun across the sky by placing an X in the center of a 12-inch (30-cm) square of cardboard. At sunrise or early morning, place the cardboard outdoors where it will receive direct sunlight during the entire day. Place the bowl from the original experiment upside down on the cardboard with the X in the center of the bowl. Starting at or near the time of sunrise, touch the glass dome with the tip of a pencil so that the shadow of the pencil's tip falls on the X mark. With the tip of a marking pen, make a dot on the glass where the tip of the pencil touches the glass. Continue making marks every hour or as often as possible throughout the day. Use a compass to determine the direction of the Sun's apparent movement.

   b. Repeat the previous experiment during different months. Take photos of the bowl after each experiment. Date the photos and use them to represent the changes in the apparent movement of the Sun during different times of the year.

2. Claudius Ptolemy was one of the great astronomers. Little is known about his life, including his birth date, but he worked in Greece around A.D. 140. It was at this time that he proposed a **geocentric** (Earth-centered) model for our solar system. According to Ptolemy, the Sun, the Moon, and the planets each move in small circles called **epicycles.** The centers of the epicycles trace out larger circles, called **deferents,** around the Earth. Near the center of all these larger circles is the Earth. Make a dia-

PTOLEMY'S GEOCENTRIC MODEL

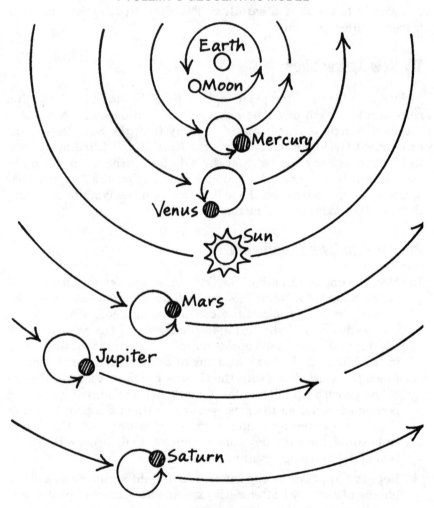

Figure 4.2

gram similar to Figure 4.2 showing Ptolemy's model of the geocentric solar system. Note that a line drawn from the Earth to the Sun would pass through the centers of the epicycles of Mercury and Venus. This is how Ptolemy explained the fact that these planets always appear near the Sun.

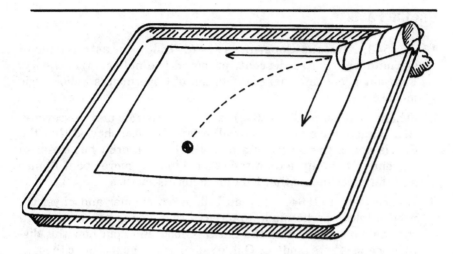

Figure 4.3

3. Sir Isaac Newton (1642–1727), an English scientist, determined that planets move in orbits around the Sun because of gravitational attraction between the Sun and each planet. Model how **gravity** (the force that pulls celestial bodies toward each other) keeps planets and other satellites in orbit around the Sun. Lay a cookie sheet on a table. Place a toilet tissue tube in one corner of the cookie sheet so that one end of the tube rests on the rim of one short side of the pan. Secure the raised end of the tube to the rim of the pan with tape. Lay a piece of typing paper in the pan so that the untaped end of the tube rests on the edge of the paper. Prop up the long side of the pan nearest the tube about 1 inch (2.5 cm) by placing a lump of clay under each corner of the long side. Fill a cup one-quarter full with water, and add 10 or more drops of red food coloring. Stir. Wet a marble with the colored water, place the marble in the tube, and release it. The marble follows a curved path because it has two directions of motion, as shown by the arrows in Figure 4.3: forward because of the slanted tube and down because gravity pulls it down the raised pan. Draw the force arrows on the paper. Photograph the setup before and after releasing the marble. Use the photographs and the paper to show the direction of the forces on the marble and the resulting curved path.

Get the Facts

1. In 1543, Nicolaus Copernicus (1473–1543), an astronomer of German and Polish descent, proposed the heliocentric theory. Find out about and make a diagram of Copernicus's heliocentric model.

2. Johannes Kepler (1571–1630), a German astronomer, discovered that planets have elliptical (oval) orbits. He also showed that the Sun is not in the center of a planet's elliptical orbit but closer to one end of the ellipse than the other. Find out more about Kepler and the experiments that led him to his discoveries.

3. Galileo Galilei (1564–1642), an Italian astronomer and physicist, used a telescope he made to observe that Venus passes through the same phases as does the Earth's Moon. Find out how this discovery and others made by Galileo support the heliocentric theory.

Night Light: The Structure and Movement of the Earth's Moon

5

The different shapes of the Moon as seen from the Earth are caused by different parts of the Moon's surface being illuminated by the Sun. The different Moon shapes are called phases, and all are seen during a period of time called a synodic month.

In this project, you will use the apparent distance to the Moon to experimentally calculate the diameter of the Moon. You will use the known average diameter of the Moon to calculate the percentage of error of your measurements. You will photograph the phases of the Moon and determine the approximate time of moonrise for each phase.

Getting Started

Purpose: To experimentally calculate the diameter of the Moon.

Materials

scissors	yardstick (meterstick)
ruler	transparent tape
index card	chair
paper hole punch	calculator

Note: This experiment must be performed outdoors on a clear night with a full moon.

Procedure

1. Cut a 1 × 2-inch (2.54 × 5.08-cm) piece from the index card.

2. Using the paper hole punch, cut a hole in the center of the card. The round hole in the center should have a diameter of ¼ inch (0.635 cm). The diameter of the hole, ¼ inch (0.635 cm), will be the apparent diameter of the Moon and will be called D_2.

3. Lay about ½ inch (1.27 cm) of one short end of the card on the zero end of the yardstick (meterstick). Tape the card to the stick and fold the card so that it stands upright, perpendicular to and even with the end of the stick.

4. Outside during a clear night with a full moon, lay the stick over the back of a chair, aiming the end with the card at the Moon.

5. Kneel by the chair with the edge of the stick next to the side of your face (see Figure 5.1).

6. Close one eye, keeping the eye next to the stick open. Look at the Moon through the hole in the card.

7. Move the stick toward, then away from, the Moon until the diameter of the Moon exactly fills the hole in the card. Record the measurement on the stick that is even with your open eye. This is the apparent distance to the Moon and will be called d_2. Note that the known average distance to the Moon, called d_1, is 235,000 miles (376,000 km).

8. Use the equation below to calculate the diameter of the Moon, which will be called D_1.

$$D_1/D_2 = d_1/d_2$$

where
D_1 = calculated diameter of the Moon
D_2 = apparent diameter of the Moon = width of the hole in the card = ¼ inch, or 0.25 inch (0.635 cm)
d_1 = known average distance to the Moon = 235,000 miles (376,000 km)
d_2 = apparent distance to the Moon as measured in step 7

Example:
If d_2 is 27¼ inches, or 27.25 inches (69.215 cm), then

$D_1/D_2 = d_1/d_2$
$\quad D_1 = (d_1/d_2)D_2$
$\qquad = $ (235,000 miles [376,000 km] ÷ 27.25 inches [69.215 cm])
$\qquad \quad$ × 0.25 inch (0.635 cm)
$\qquad = $ 2,155.96 miles (3,449.54 km)

Results

The experimentally calculated diameter of the Moon using the measurements in the example is 2,155.96 miles (3,449.54 km).

Figure 5.1

Why?

The equation used in this experiment is called a **proportion**, a statement of equality between two ratios. A **ratio** is a comparison of one value to another. Ratios are written as fractions. In this experiment, you used ratios to calculate the diameter of the Moon. These ratios and their proportions are written as $D_1/D_2 = d_1/d_2$, which means the ratio of the calculated diameter of the Moon, D_1, to the apparent diameter of the Moon, D_2, is equal to the ratio of the known average distance to the Moon, d_1, to the apparent distance to the Moon, d_2. From this proportion, the diameter of the Moon, D_1, is calculated to be 2,155.96 miles (3,449.54 km).

Try New Approaches

Does the position of the Moon above the horizon affect the results? Repeat the experiment twice, first measuring early in the evening when the Moon is nearer the **horizon** (a line where the sky appears to meet the Earth). Measure again later the same evening when the Moon is farther above the horizon or near its **zenith** (a celestial body's point of highest altitude in the sky). **Science Fair Hint:** Ask a helper to take a photograph of you measuring the apparent distance to the Moon. Use this and your calculations to represent the results of the experiment.

Design Your Own Experiment

1. Calculate the percentage of error of your measurements using the following example and the known average diameter of the Moon, 2,172.5 miles (3,476 km):

   Example:
   - Determine the **absolute difference** (a positive difference calculated by subtracting a smaller number from a larger number) between the known average diameter and your experimentally calculated diameter:

     absolute difference = 2,172.5 miles (3,476 km)
     $$- \ 2{,}155.96 \text{ miles } (3{,}449.54 \text{ km})$$
     $$= \quad 16.54 \text{ miles } (26.46 \text{ km})$$

   - Divide the absolute difference by the known average diameter of the Moon:

16.54 miles (26.46 km) ÷ 2,172.5 miles (3,476 km)
= 0.00761(0.00761)

- Find the percentage by multiplying the dividend by 100:

$$0.00761 \times 100 = 0.76\%$$

The percentage of error of the example measurement is 0.76%.

2. The different shapes of the Moon as seen from the Earth are called **phases**. These shapes are different amounts of illuminated moon surface and are caused by the Moon's revolving around the Earth. Take photographs or make diagrams of the Moon each night for one **synodic month** (the time between two successive new moons), 29½ days. Prepare a display with the photos or diagrams, labeling these phases: new moon, waxing crescent, first quarter, waxing gibbous, full moon, waning gibbous, last quarter, and waning crescent. For information about the Moon's phases, see Dinah Moché, *Astronomy* (New York: Wiley, 1996), pp. 196–197.

3. The Moon and the Sun both rise and set in the general direction of from east to west. In the new moon phase, the Moon rises with the Sun and travels close to it across the sky. The Moon rises about 50 minutes later each day in relation to the Sun. Table 5.1 shows the approximate time of moonrise for four moon phases during a synodic month. Use the table to prepare a diagram similar to Figure 5.2.

Table 5.1 Moonrise		
Synodic Month	Moon Phase	Approximate Time of Moonrise
day 1	new moon	sunrise
day 9	first quarter	noon
day 16	full moon	sunset
day 22	last quarter	midnight
day 30	new moon	sunrise

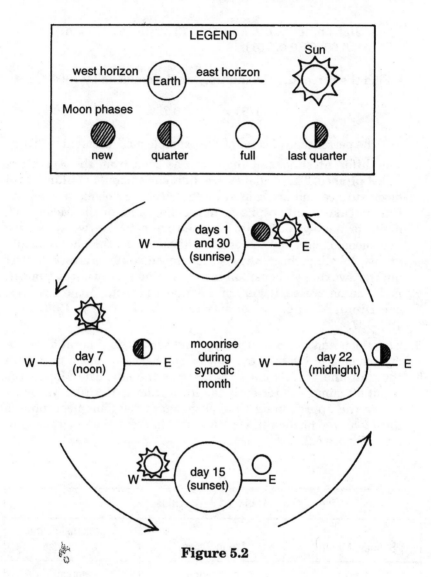

Figure 5.2

Get the Facts

The Earth and the Moon both make shadows. An *eclipse* occurs when
one celestial body passes into the shadow of another celestial body.
What are lunar and solar eclipses? During which phase of the Moon
do these eclipses occur? For information about the Moon's phases and
eclipses, see "Moon" in the *World Book Encyclopedia*.

Mobile Stars: The Apparent Movement of Stars

Stars do move through space. But, as observed from the Earth, which is also moving, the position of stars in relation to each other is generally the same. The position of all the stars in the sky appears to change from one hour to the next. This apparent change of position is due to the motion of the Earth.

In this project, you will study apparent star movement due to parallax. You will learn how parallax distance indicates the distance of stars from the Earth and how astronomers determine this distance. Stellar parallax is measured in seconds of arc, and you will get an idea of how small this measurement is. You will make a star clock to determine the direction of the apparent movement of stars during the night and from one month to the next. A method for identifying circumpolar stars at given latitudes will also be determined.

Getting Started

Purpose: To determine how the Earth's rotation makes stars appear to change position.

Materials

pencil

scissors

1-inch (2.5-cm) square of
stiff paper (index card
works well)

metric ruler

sheet of typing paper

two marble-size pieces of
modeling clay

Procedure

1. Draw a five-pointed 1 × 1-inch (2.5 × 2.5-cm) star on the stiff paper square. Cut out the star.

2. Use the ruler to draw a straight line from top to bottom down the center of the sheet of typing paper.

3. Lay the paper on the edge of a table with the line perpendicular to the table's edge.

43

Figure 6.1

4. Use one of the clay pieces to stand the ruler on edge parallel to the edge of the paper with the metric measurements at the top and the 15-cm mark of the ruler at the end of the line on the paper.

5. Stand the star upright in the second piece of clay with the legs of the star in the clay and its point up.

6. Set the star in the center of the line on the paper.

7. Kneel beside the table with your nose at the end of the line on the paper.

8. Close your right eye and using your left eye observe the position of the star against the ruler behind it (see Figure 6.1). Read the measurement on the ruler behind the tip of the star's top point.

9. Without moving your head, open your right eye and close your left eye. With your right eye, again read the measurement on the ruler behind the tip of the star's top point.

10. Calculate the absolute difference between the readings in steps 8 and 9 by subtracting the smaller number from the larger one.

Example:

$$16.7 \text{ cm} - 13.1 \text{ cm} = 3.6 \text{ cm}$$

Results

The star appears to move first to the right, then to the left. In the example, the distance between the star's two apparent positions is 3.6 cm.

Why?

A straight line drawn between the two points from which an object is observed is called a **baseline**. In this experiment, the position of each eye represents the different positions of the Earth during its rotation around the Sun. This is much like observing the stars from the Earth at different points along its orbit. The baseline is an imaginary line between your eyes, as your eyes sight the star from two different points (see Figure 6.2). Each eye sees the star from a different angle; thus each eye sees a different background behind the star. The star seems to move from its actual location. The apparent change in the position of an object when viewed from two different points is called **parallax**. In the example, the star's **parallax distance** (linear distance between the apparent positions of an object due to parallax) is 3.6 cm.

Try New Approaches

1. How does the distance of a star from the Earth affect its parallax distance? Show how the parallax distance of stars at different distances from the Earth can be compared. Repeat the experiment three times, with the star at 5 cm, 10 cm, and 25 cm from the edge of the paper nearest your eyes. Mark these locations along the line on the paper. Without moving your head during the experiment, have a helper put the star on the 5-cm mark. Sight the star, then have your helper record the measurements and move the star to the 10-cm mark. Sight the star as before, then repeat for

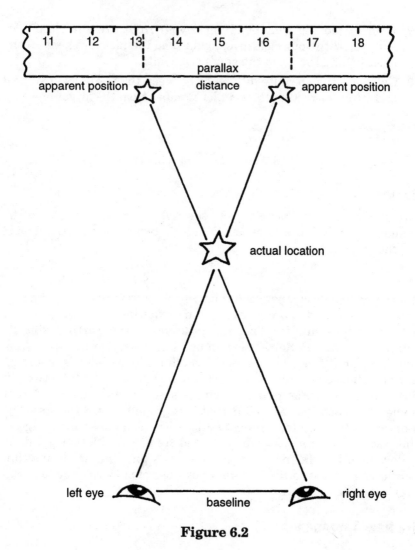

Figure 6.2

the 25-cm mark. **Science Fair Hint:** Use diagrams of each measurement, like the one in Figure 6.2, to compare the parallax distances of stars at different distances from the Earth.

2. How does the length of the baseline affect the parallax distance? Repeat the experiment, first looking at the star with your right eye from the right corner of the paper next to table's edge. Then look at the star with your left eye from the left corner of the paper. Compare the parallax distance in this experiment with that of the original experiment.

Design Your Own Experiment

1. Astronomers use the parallax angle of stars close to the Earth to determine the stars' distance from Earth. The **parallax angle** (**p**) of a star is called its **stellar parallax** and is one-half of the star's total angular shift when observed from opposite sides of the Earth's orbit around the Sun. To measure the parallax of a star, astronomers photograph the sky on one night, then photograph it again six months later when the Earth is on the opposite side of its orbit. This provides the longest baseline, with viewing spots separated by a distance equal to the diameter of the Earth's orbit around the Sun, about 187 million miles (300 million km). A comparison of the two photographs shows that the other stars seen with the sighted star are different in each photo. Prepare a drawing similar to the one in Figure 6.3, which shows the parallax angle (*p*) when photos are taken from opposite sides of the Earth's orbit.

2a. In the Northern Hemisphere, stars appear to move around **Polaris** (the North Star, located above the Earth's north axis). This apparent movement is due to the rotation of the Earth on its axis. Stars that never sink below the horizon of the observer but appear to revolve around a point in the sky above the Earth's axis are called **circumpolar stars**. At latitudes of 40° N or greater, the stars in the Big Dipper's bowl are circumpolar and appear to revolve around Polaris.

   Prepare a star clock to observe the apparent movement of the Big Dipper's stars by drawing two circles on stiff paper, such as a file folder. Make the diameter of one circle 8 inches (20 cm) and the diameter of the second circle 6 inches (15 cm). Use a paper punch to make a hole in the center of each circle. Draw a star, Polaris, in the center of the small circle and the stars of the Big Dipper near the circumference, as shown in Figure 6.4. Add a dashed line from Polaris through the two stars in the Big Dipper's bowl and to the circumference. Mark an arrow at the end of this line. Lay the small circle in the center of the large circle. Insert a paper brad through the center of the two circles, then write "Facing North" and the directions "West" and "East" along the circumference of the large circle.

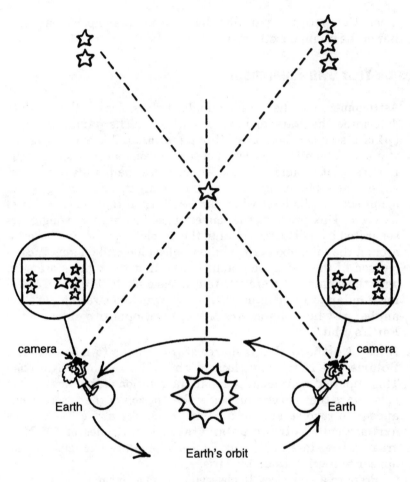

Figure 6.3

On a clear, dark night, go outdoors. Use a compass to find
north or, if you do not have a compass, face in the direction that
the sun rises each day, then turn your head and look in the direction of your left shoulder. This is approximately north. Hold the
circles in front of you with the direction "Facing North" at the
bottom. Find the Big Dipper in the northern sky and turn the
small circle so that in relation to the northern horizon the position of the Big Dipper on the paper matches the position of the
Big Dipper in the sky. Use an astronomer's flashlight (see
Appendix 3) to view the circles. On the large circle, make a mark

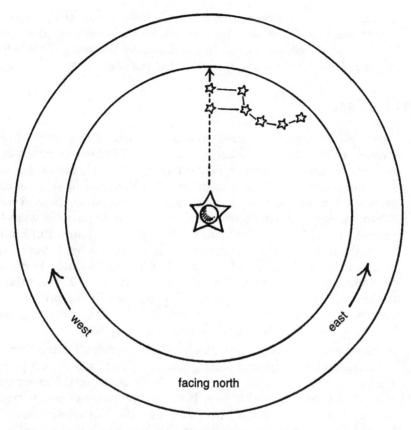

Figure 6.4

at the end of the arrow and record the time and date. Repeat this every hour for as many hours as possible during the night. Use the paper model to determine the direction of the apparent movement of stars due to the Earth's rotation. *Note:* If you live at a latitude south of 40° N, use a single circumpolar star in the Big Dipper or in the constellation Cepheus.

For information on circumpolar stars, see *Janice VanCleave's Constellations for Every Kid* (New York: Wiley, 1997), pp. 45–55.

b. The movement of the Earth around the Sun results in the rising of the stars about 4 minutes earlier each evening. Four minutes each day for 30 days is 120 minutes, or 2 hours; thus the stars rise about 2 hours earlier each month. As a result, the position of stars at the same time of night changes slightly each night. This is a noticeable change from month to month. Repeat the previous experiment at the same time of night once a month for as many months as possible to compare the changing positions of the Big Dipper. Use the models to represent the results.

Get the Facts

1. The parallax angle is so small that it is measured in a unit called *seconds of arc*. The thickness of a page in this book is about 30 seconds of arc. The Earth's nearest star, Alpha Centauri, has a parallax angle of 0.73 second of arc. The distance to stars is so great that a special unit of measure called the *parsec* is used for it. One parsec is the distance a star would be if its parallax were 1 second of arc. One parsec is equal to 3.26 light-years. Find out more about measuring star distances. How far is a light-year? Up to what distance can the stellar parallax method accurately measure the distance of stars? For information about stellar parallax, see Dinah Moché, *Astronomy* (New York: Wiley, 1996), pp. 62–63, or look up "parsec" in the *Astronomy Facts on File Dictionary* by Valerie Illingworth (New York: Facts on File, 1994).

2. Stars appear to be on an imaginary sphere surrounding the Earth called the *celestial sphere,* which, like the Earth, has an equator. The location of a star in degrees north or south of the celestial equator is called its *declination.* How can the range of declination for northern circumpolar stars at a specific latitude be determined? For information, see *Janice VanCleave's Constellations for Every Kid* (New York: Wiley, 1997), pp. 45–46.

7 | Time: Day Lengths and Time Zones

Sidereal time and solar time are the systems used for measuring the passage of time. While these systems only vary by about 4 minutes, this small difference is significant when considering long spans of time.

In this project, you will model Earth's movement during one sidereal day and one solar day to compare the differences between these two time measurements. You will calculate the angular difference between the position of a meridian at noon on a sidereal day and on a solar day. You will design a map showing the Earth's time zones. You will learn about the difference between local "sun time" and standard time, and how to experimentally determine the difference where you live.

Getting Started

Purpose: To model a sidereal day.

Materials

marker	toothpick
sheet of typing paper	pencil
ruler	flashlight
lemon-size piece of modeling clay	

Procedure

1. Place the paper sideways, and draw a 6-inch (15-cm) horizontal line across the center of the paper. Label the line A. Two inches (5 cm) above this line, center a second line that is 5 inches (7.5 cm) long and label it B.

2. Shape the clay into a sphere.

3. Use the pencil to draw two circles around the clay sphere. Make the two circles perpendicular to each other at the top and bottom of the sphere.

4. Break the toothpick in half.

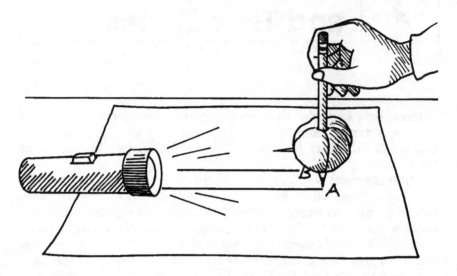

Figure 7.1

5. Insert one of the broken ends of the toothpick into the center of one of the four line segments drawn on the sphere. Discard the other half of the toothpick.

6. Insert the pencil through the clay sphere from top to bottom until just its tip sticks out the bottom.

7. Lay the paper on the table so that the labeled ends of the lines are to the right. Turn on the flashlight and place it at the left end of line A.

8. Hold the pencil and position the clay sphere at the right end of line A so that the toothpick is parallel with the line and points toward the flashlight (see Figure 7.1).

9. Holding the pencil, rotate the sphere counterclockwise one whole turn as you move the sphere to the right end of line B. Position the sphere so that the toothpick is parallel with line B. Observe the direction the toothpick points in relation to the flashlight.
Note: Keep the paper, flashlight, and sphere for the following experiment.

Results

Moving from line A to line B, the sphere makes one complete rotation. The toothpick points toward the flashlight when the sphere is at the end of line A, but doesn't point toward the flashlight when the sphere is at the end of line B.

Why?

The circles on the clay sphere represent meridians on the Earth. The toothpick is used to mark one of the meridians so its position and movement can be tracked. When the sphere is on line A and the toothpick points toward the flashlight, the meridian is in line with the Sun and the time is twelve o'clock in the daytime, or **noon**. At noon, the Sun crosses the local meridian and is at its zenith. The turning of the clay and the movement of the sphere from line A to line B represent the Earth's rotation on its axis and movement along its orbit around the Sun during one **sidereal day** (time it takes for a celestial body to make one complete rotation on its axis). A sidereal day for Earth is about 23 hours 56 minutes.

The sphere, like the Earth, must make slightly more than one whole turn before it points toward the Sun and it is noon again for any one meridian. To an observer on Earth, it appears that the Sun moves across the sky. Thus a **solar day** can be defined as the interval from the time the Sun crosses a meridian on Earth to the time the Sun returns to that meridian. In other words, it is the time period from noon of one day until noon of the next day. For timekeeping, we use an average of the solar days over a year, called a **mean solar day**, which is equal to 24 hours.

Try New Approaches

1a. Demonstrate a solar day by repeating steps 7 through 9, but continue rotating the clay sphere until the toothpick points toward the flashlight. **Science Fair Hint:** Take a photograph of the position of the clay sphere at the end of step 8 with the sphere on line A and the toothpick pointing toward the flashlight. This photograph represents the position of a meridian at noon, the starting of a time period. Take a second photo after step 9 of the original experiment, when the toothpick is parallel with line B. This second photograph represents the position of the meridian at the end of one sidereal day. Take a third photo after step 9 of the repeated experiment, when the toothpick points toward the flashlight. This photo represents the position of the meridian at the end of one solar day. Use these photos to compare the positions of a meridian during one sidereal day and one solar day.

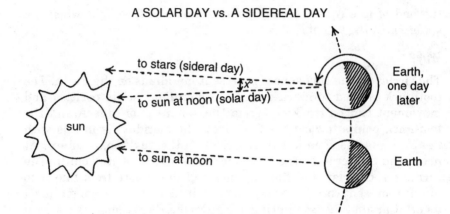

Figure 7.2

b. The clay model greatly exaggerates the angular difference between the position of a meridian at noon on the end of a sidereal day and on a solar day. Calculate this difference (*x*) using the following facts:

- The time difference between a sidereal day and a solar day is about 4 minutes.
- Earth rotates 360° in about 23 hours 56 minutes.

First change sidereal time to minutes (23 hours × 60 minutes/hour + 56 minutes = 1,436 minutes), then use the following equation:

$$x/4 \text{ minutes} = 360°/1,436 \text{ minutes}$$
$$x = 360°/1,436 \text{ minutes} \times 4 \text{ minutes}$$
$$= ? \text{ degrees}$$

Science Fair Hint: Make a diagram representing the angular difference between a sidereal day and a solar day, similar to Figure 7.2, replacing *x*° with your calculation for the angular measurement.

Design Your Own Experiment

Earth is divided into 24 internationally agreed **time zones**. Each time zone is about 15° of longitude wide, and local time is the same throughout a given time zone. Each zone is centered on a meridian called the **time meridian**, with about 7.5° of longitude on each side of the meridian. The clock time within each time zone is called **standard time**. Standard time for each time zone is based on the mean solar time of the time meridian of the zone. The prime meridian (0°) is the reference line for standard time. Time at the prime meridian is called **Greenwich Mean Time**, or **GMT**. GMT applies 7.5° east and west of the prime meridian. Each time meridian 15° east or west of the prime meridian marks a time difference of 1 hour. Time zones west of the prime meridian are earlier than GMT, and those east of it are later than GMT.

Design a map showing time zones of the Earth. Find out what and where the international date line is. For more information about time zones, see *Janice VanCleave's Geography for Every Kid* (New York: Wiley, 1993), pp. 135–144.

Get the Facts

1. The Earth is not a perfect sphere, so it wobbles as it rotates on its axis. This wobble is called *precession,* and the length of time it takes the Earth to make one complete precession is called a *platonic year.* How long is a platonic year? For information about the Earth's precession, see H. A. Rey, *The Stars* (Boston: Houghton Mifflin, 1976), pp. 127–129.

2. The Sun appears to move fastest during January and slowest during July. Thus, noon as determined by sun time is faster than standard clock time on some days and slower on other days. What causes this change in the Sun's motion? What is True Sun? Average Sun or Mean Sun? What is an analemma? How can you determine the difference between sun time and standard time where you live? For information, see Philip Harrington and Edward Pascuzzi, *Astronomy for All Ages* (Old Saybrook, Conn.: Globe Pequot Press, 1994), pp. 89–95.

Early Methods: Ancient Techniques of Determining Earth's Size and Shape

8

In ancient times many natural phenomena were explained by weaving myths about what was observed. As time passed, more practical applications were based on observations, such as using stars as points of reference when traveling. The Greeks were noted for applications of geometric measurement that were amazingly accurate in describing the size and motion of the Earth and other planets.

In this project, you will calculate the circumference and radius of a circle using the geometric method Eratosthenes used to determine the circumference and radius of the Earth. You will learn how to calculate the angle of a shadow. Following Eratosthenes' example of using the difference in the angle of shadows cast in different cities at the same hour, you will determine the circumference of the Earth for yourself. You will learn how a lunar eclipse was used to verify the shape of the Earth.

Getting Started

Purpose: To learn Eratosthenes' geometric method of determining the arc between two cities on the same meridian.

Materials

roll of masking tape
scissors
sheet of typing paper

pen
metric ruler
protractor

Procedure

1. Lay the roll of tape flat in the center of the paper and trace around it with the pen.

2. Find the center of the circle drawn on the paper by folding the circle in half twice: first fold the circle from top to bottom, then fold again from side to side.

3. Unfold the paper and mark a point in the center where the fold lines cross. Label this point *A*.

4. Lay the ruler across the circle with its bottom edge on the horizontal fold line.

5. Mark two points on the circumference of the circle where the top and bottom edges of the ruler touch the one side of the circle. Label the points *B* and *C*, as shown in Figure 8.1.

6. Use the ruler to draw a line from point *A* to each of the points *B* and *C*. Extend the lines 5 cm or more outside the perimeter of the circle to points *D* and *F* (see Figure 8.1).

7. From points *B* and *D*, draw lines perpendicular to the circle and parallel to line *FC*. Mark point *E* as shown.

8. Use the protractor to measure the angles between angle *CAB* and *EBD* (see Figure 8.1).

Results

The degrees of an arc are determined.

Why?

Eratosthenes (276–194 B.C.), a librarian at the museum in Alexandria, Egypt, used a geometric method similar to the one in this experiment to determine the degrees of **arc** (part of a circle) between two cities, Syene (Aswan) and Alexandria. He believed that the Earth is a sphere. His method involved using the difference in the angle of shadows cast at the same hour in the cities. Eratosthenes learned that at noon on the summer solstice (June 21), the Sun's reflection could be seen in the water at the bottom of a well in Syene (Aswan). This meant that the Sun was exactly overhead at that time and no shadows were cast. Thus, the Sun's rays were perpendicular to the well and in line with the radius of the Earth, represented by line *CA* in this experiment. He observed that at the same time in Alexandria, a tall pillar cast a shadow. Eratosthenes knew that the pillar was perpendicular to the Earth's surface and thus in line with the radius of the Earth. Since sunlight comes from such a great distance, sun rays are parallel to each other when they reach the Earth. Because the Earth's surface is curved, there is an angle between the pillar and the parallel Sun's rays. This angle is represented by the shadow

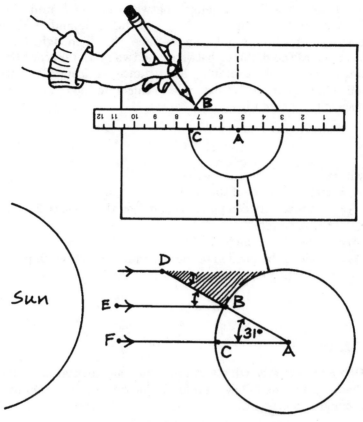

Figure 8.1

angle in this experiment, which is equal to angle *EBD* and angle *CAB* at the center of the circle. With this information, he determined the angle of the arc between Syene and Alexandria using the angle of the pillar's shadow. In this experiment, angle *CAB*, angle *EBD*, and the shadow's angle are 31°, but the angle measured by Eratosthenes was only 7°. Thus, the arc between the two cities was determined to be 7°.

Try New Approaches

1a. The degrees of arc and the **arc length** (length of a portion of the circumference of a circle) can be used to determine the circumference of a circle. Determine the circumference of the roll of tape.

First measure the arc length between points B and C in the drawing by laying the roll of tape on the circle and marking the positions of points B and C on the tape. Unroll enough of the tape to measure the distance between the two marks. Record this distance as d_2. In the example, this distance is 2.9 cm. Then, use the following equation and example to calculate the outer circumference of the roll of tape:

$$d_1/d_2 = A_1/A_2$$

where
d_1 = circumference of the circle
d_2 = distance between points B and C on the circle (= 2.9 cm in this example)
A_1 = angle of a circle (= 360°)
A_2 = angle of the portion of the circumference between points B and C (= 31° in this example)

$$d_1 = (A_1/A_2)d_2$$
$$= (360°/31°)2.9 \text{ cm}$$
$$= 33.7 \text{ cm}$$

b. Determine the Earth's circumference as calculated by Eratosthenes using the following information *and* the equation from the previous experiment.

d_1 = circumference of the Earth
d_2 = distance from Syene to Alexandria (= 500 miles ([800 km])
A_1 = angle of a circle (= 360°)
A_2 = angle of the portion of the arc between Syene and Alexandria (7°)

2a. Eratosthenes knew that the circumference of a circle is about 3.14 times as great as its diameter. The Greeks called this number **pi**, which is written π. He used pi and the fact that the diameter of a circle is twice its radius to calculate the Earth's radius. Use the following equation and example *and* the circumference from the previous experiment to determine the Earth's radius as calculated by Eratosthenes:

$$d_1 = 2\pi r$$

where
d_1 = circumference of the circle (= 33.7 cm in the original experiment)
$\pi = 3.14$
r = radius of the circle

$$r = d_1/2\pi$$
$$= 33.7 \text{ cm} /(2 \times 3.14)$$
$$= 5.37 \text{ cm}$$

b. Determine the Earth's radius as calculated by Eratosthenes using the following information and the equation from the previous experiment.

d_1 = circumference of the Earth (calculated in part 1a)
r = radius of the Earth
$\pi = 3.14$

3. Eratosthenes calculated the Earth's **polar circumference**, the distance around the Earth from Pole to Pole. This circumference is now known to be about 24,951 miles (39,922 km), and the radius is about 3,973 miles (6,357 km). Use these figures and the information in Chapter 5, "Night Light: The Structure and Movement of the Earth's Moon," to calculate the percentage of error for Eratosthenes' calculations for the Earth's circumference and radius.

Design Your Own Experiment

1. Demonstrate how the angle of a shadow is calculated. Tape a ruler to the side of a wooden block so that the ruler stands vertical. Set the block outdoors on level ground and use a carpenter's level to ensure that the block is level. Tape a string to the top of the ruler, and without moving the ruler, have a helper stretch the string between the top of the ruler and the end of the ruler's shadow. Use a protractor to measure the angle between the ruler and the string, as shown in Figure 8.2.

2. Use Eratosthenes' method to measure the circumference of the Earth yourself, using a helper who lives several hundred miles (km) due north or south of you. First, use an atlas to determine the longitude and latitude of your town. Then find a town on the

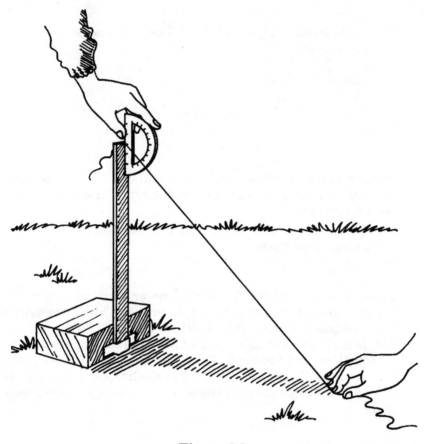

Figure 8.2

same longitude about 5° to 10° of latitude north or south. Use the scale on the map to determine the exact distance in miles. If you do not know anyone who lives in that town, with adult assistance you might be able to find someone via the World Wide Web. Design a way to measure the angle of the shadow, or use the method from the previous experiment. You must measure the angle of the shadow at the same hour. Try to do it on the same day or within the same week. Determine the absolute difference of the angle of the two shadows by subtracting the smaller angle from the larger angle. Use the equation from the original experiment to calculate the circumference of the Earth.

Take measurements two to three different times during the day and average the circumferences from your results. Repeat the procedure with a helper in another town in the opposite direction. Compare your measurements to the modern measurement of the Earth's circumference, calculating your percentage of error. Make and display diagrams showing the angles of the shadow measured by Eratosthenes and those measured by you and your helpers.

Get the Facts

1. Eratosthenes' calculations were replaced by less accurate measurements promoted by Ptolemy (second century A.D.), an Alexandrian scholar. Ptolemy calculated the circumference to be about 18,000 miles (28,800 km). Because of this inaccurate measurement, Christopher Columbus (1451–1506) sailed west thinking the Earth was much smaller than it really is. What was the system of measurement promoted by Ptolemy? For information about early measurements of the Earth's circumference, see John Farndon, *How the Earth Works* (New York: Reader's Digest Association, 1992), p. 22.

2. Some early astronomers thought the Earth to be a flat square under a pyramid-shaped sky, and others believed it to be a plate resting on the backs of four elephants standing on a giant floating turtle. Find out more about the early views of the shape of the Earth and its place in the universe. Make and display diagrams of some of the early views. How was a lunar eclipse used to prove the Earth is round? For information, see *How the Earth Works*, pp. 12–13, 24.

Part Three

Physical Composition of the Earth

Elements: The Earth's Building Blocks

9

The Earth is made of matter, which exists as solid, liquid, or gas and is made up of tiny particles called atoms. Matter with only one kind of atom is an element, and the combination of elements forms compounds. Elements or compounds may be blended to form mixtures. Elements, compounds, and mixtures are the building blocks of the Earth.

In this project, you will construct pie charts showing the different elements that make up each of the three outer parts of the Earth, lithosphere, hydrosphere, and atmosphere, and the salt compounds in seawater. You will learn how elements combine to form compounds and model the attraction that holds compounds together. You will also learn about and model the changes in the phases of matter.

Getting Started

Purpose: To construct pie charts to represent the most abundant substances in the Earth's lithosphere.

Materials

pen

sheet of typing paper

drawing compass

ruler

protractor with 6-inch (15-cm) base

Procedure

1. Write the title "Elements of the Earth's Lithosphere" at the top of the paper.

2. Use the compass to draw a 6-inch (15-cm) circle below the title.

3. The element oxygen makes up about 47% of the elements in the Earth's lithosphere. A pie chart contains 360°. Thus, oxygen would be represented on the pie chart by an arc equal to 47% of

360°. Calculate this, rounding the answer to the nearest whole number.

Example:

$$x = 47\% \times 360°$$

Note: To change a percent number to a decimal number, move the decimal to the left two places and remove the percent sign.

$$x = 0.47 \times 360°$$
$$= 169.2°$$
$$= 169°$$

4. Draw the 169° angle of arc on the circle by first drawing a horizontal line from the left side of the circumference to the center of the circle.
5. Position the protractor on this line and mark 169° as accurately as possible on the circumference.
6. Remove the protractor and draw a line from the center of the circle to the 169° mark. Label this area of the pie chart "Oxygen 47%."
7. The element silicon makes up about 28% of the Earth's lithosphere. Calculate the angle of arc using the equation in step 3:

$$x = 0.28 \times 360°$$
$$= 100.8°$$
$$= 101°$$

8. Position the protractor on the line drawn in step 6 for oxygen, then mark 101° on the circumference.
9. Label this area of the pie chart "Silicon 28%."
10. The rest of the lithosphere is made up of other elements. Calculate the remaining percentage by adding the known percentages together and subtracting from 100%:

$$47\% + 28\% = 75\%$$
$$100\% - 75\% = 25\%$$

11. Complete the pie chart by labeling the remaining area "Other Elements 25%," as shown in Figure 9.1.

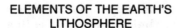

ELEMENTS OF THE EARTH'S
LITHOSPHERE

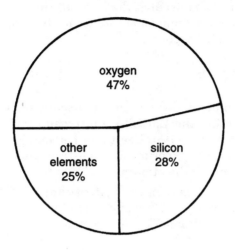

oxygen
47%

other
elements
25%

silicon
28%

Figure 9.1

Results

A pie chart is made showing percentages of the two most abundant elements in the Earth's lithosphere.

Why?

The Earth's **lithosphere** starts at its surface and extends to a depth of about 62.5 miles (100 km). **Matter** is any substance that has **mass** (the amount of material in a substance) and occupies space. Matter is made of **atoms** (smallest particles of an element that retain the properties of that element), which include **electrons** (negatively charged subatomic particles), **protons** (positively charged subatomic particles), and **neutrons** (neutrally charged subatomic particles). Matter made of atoms that are all alike is an **element**. There are 92 naturally occurring elements on Earth. Eight of these elements make up about 98% of the mass of the Earth's lithosphere. The pie chart shows that three-fourths (75%) of the Earth's lithosphere is made of just the elements oxygen and silicon. Silicon and oxygen combine with other kinds of atoms to form **molecules** (a combination of two or more atoms) called **silicates**. The attraction between atoms in a molecule that keeps them together is called a **chemical bond**. Matter made up of molecules that are all alike is a **compound**. Silicates are the most common substance in the rocky material making up the Earth's lithosphere.

Try New Approaches

1. The most abundant elements in the **atmosphere** (gaseous envelope surrounding the Earth) are nitrogen (78%), oxygen (21%), and other elements (1%). Use these percentages and the procedure in the original experiment to construct a pie chart representing the elements in the atmosphere.

2. The abundant elements in the **hydrosphere** (total watery part of the Earth) are oxygen (86%) and hydrogen (11%). Other elements make up the remaining 3%. Construct a pie chart showing the elements in the hydrosphere.

Design Your Own Experiment

Within the lithosphere, most elements are joined together to form **minerals** (natural substances with specific chemical compositions and distinct atomic structures). A few minerals occur as just one element, such as when carbon atoms join to form the mineral graphite. Make a model of graphite using clay balls for atoms and toothpicks for chemical bonds. Start by using six clay balls and six toothpicks to form a hexagon to represent a carbon atom. Add four more clay balls and toothpicks to form a single layer made up of two hexagons joined together. Make another layer of two hexagons and stack the second layer on top of the first one using five 6-inch (15-cm) pieces of spaghetti (see Figure 9.2).

In graphite layers, **covalent bonds** (strong attractions between atoms that share electrons) hold the carbon atoms within the layers together. In this experiment, toothpicks represent covalent bonds. One layer of graphite is held to another graphite layer by **van der Waals bonds** (weak electrostatic attractions between atoms that are easily broken). The spaghetti represents these weak bonds. What is the difference between these types of bonds? For information, see Brian J. Skinner and Stephen C. Porter, *The Dynamic Earth* (New York: Wiley, 1992), pp. 47–48.

covalent bonds   carbon atoms

Van der
Waals
bonds

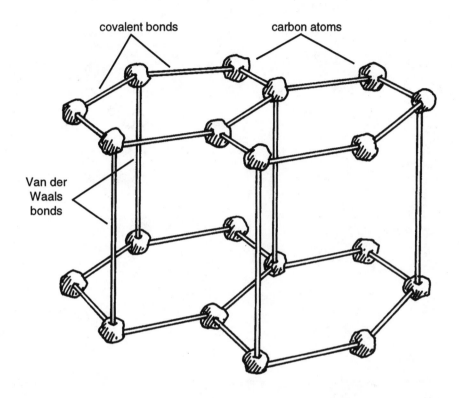

Figure 9.2

Get the Facts

Matter exists in three basic *phases:* solid, liquid, and gas. The atoms in a solid vibrate but are held in relatively fixed positions. A solid has a definite shape and volume. Use a chemistry or earth science textbook to discover the movement, shape, and volume of the atoms of liquids and gases. What causes matter to change from one phase to another? Use this information to model and explain phase changes in the Earth's lithosphere, hydrosphere, and atmosphere, such as the evaporation of water from the hydrosphere and the condensation of water in the atmosphere in the formation of clouds and precipitation. Display models showing the bonding between the three phases of matter.

The Earth's Layers: Chemical and Physical Properties of the Earth

10

The different chemicals making up the layers of the Earth are not evenly distributed. Specific groups of chemicals are believed to be found at the Earth's surface and at different depths below its surface. Thus, the Earth has layers with different chemical compositions.

In this project, you will study and make models of the layers of the Earth as classified by their chemical composition and phase composition. You will calculate the radius or thickness of the Earth's layers as a percentage of the Earth's radius and design a pie chart to show these percentages. You will examine the relation of depth to temperature of the Earth's layers and prepare a table and a graph representing this relation.

Getting Started

Purpose: To make a model of the Earth's three layers based on chemical composition.

Materials

drawing compass

metric ruler

6-inch (15-cm) square of cardboard

three lemon-size pieces of modeling clay: one yellow, one red, and one blue

12-inch (30-cm) piece of string

Procedure

1. Use the compass to draw a 6.8-cm-diameter circle in the center of the cardboard.

2. Draw a second circle around the first one with a diameter of 12.6 cm. The circumference of this circle will be 2.9 cm from the circumference of the inner circle.

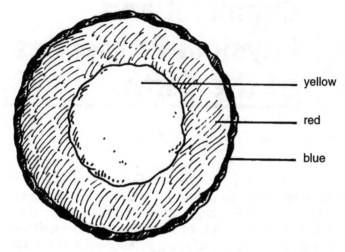

Figure 10.1

3. Fill the inner circle with yellow clay and the outer circle with red clay.

4. Use the blue clay to make an outline as thin as possible around the circle of red clay (see Figure 10.1).

Results

A circular model with three colored layers is formed. The yellow inner layer has a diameter of 6.8 cm, the red layer is 2.9 cm thick, and the blue layer is very thin.

Why?

The three layers of clay represent the three layers of the Earth according to their chemical composition. **Chemical composition** refers to the elements and compounds that are present. The yellow inner layer of clay represents the Earth's **core** (the innermost layer of the Earth). The core is believed to be made mostly of two metals, iron and nickel. With a scale of 1 cm = 1,000 km (625 miles), a diameter of 6.8 cm represents 6,800 km (4,259 miles), which is the average diameter of the Earth's core. The core's thickness is equal to its radius, which is one-half its diameter, or 3,400 km (2,125 miles).

Surrounding the core is the **mantle**. This layer has a thickness of about 2,900 km (1,812 miles), thus the red clay representing this layer is 2.9 cm thick. The most common chemicals found in this layer are silicates, which are made of the elements silicon and oxygen combined with another element. The silicates in this layer are mostly combined with the elements iron and magnesium.

The outer layer of the Earth is called the **crust**. This is the layer you live on. Like the mantle, the crust contains large quantities of silicates. The elements combined with the silicates in the crust are largely aluminum, iron, and magnesium. This thin outer layer varies from about 5 to 50 km (3 to 30 miles) in thickness.

Try New Approaches

As a result of pressure and temperature, chemicals can be in a solid, liquid, or gas state. These forms of matter are called **phases**. On the surface, the Earth is solid, but deep inside the Earth, temperatures are great enough to melt all solid material. While the temperature can melt the solid, in much of the Earth's interior, high pressures do not allow the matter to melt. The balance between temperature and pressure in the Earth's interior varies. Thus, depending on this balance, layers of the Earth can be solid, liquid, or in between. The Earth can be divided into five layers, based on their **phase composition** (the phase of matter that is present). These five layers are the lithosphere (solid crust and uppermost part of the mantle), the **asthenosphere** (semiliquid layer of the mantle below the lithosphere), the **mesosphere** (solid remaining layer of the mantle below the asthenosphere), the **outer core** (liquid layer below the mesosphere), and the **inner core** (solid center of the Earth). Repeat the experiment making a model showing these five layers. With a pencil point, draw the boundaries of each layer in the clay. Use toothpicks and round labels to number the layers. Prepare a stand-up legend to identify the names that each number represents. **Science Fair Hint:** Make labels and a legend for the model in the original experiment. Display the models and legends from both experiments.

Design Your Own Experiment

1. Design a pie chart to represent the thickness of each of the three layers of the Earth—crust, mantle, and core—classified by chemical composition. Express each layer as a percentage of the Earth's equatorial radius, which is 6,378 km (3,986 miles). Use the following equation to determine these percentages:

$$x = T \div r \times 100$$

where
x = layer's thickness as a percentage of the Earth's radius
T = layer's thickness
r = radius of the Earth (= 6,378 km or 3,986 miles)

Example:
Calculate the thickness of the core (T = 3,400 km, or 2,125 miles) as a percentage of the Earth's radius.

$$x = 3,400 \text{ km} \div 6,378 \text{ km} \times 100$$
$$= 53.33\%$$

Use the procedure in Chapter 9, "Elements: The Earth's Building Blocks," to construct the pie chart.

2. The outer layer of the Earth is cool in comparison to its inner layers. Below the crust, the temperature continues to increase, with the core's temperature estimated to be more than 7,232°F (4,000°C). Use an earth science textbook or other books to determine the estimated temperature at different depths. Prepare a table like Table 10.1 and a line graph like Figure 10.2 showing the depths and temperatures. Explain where the fastest and slowest changes of temperature occur.

Table 10.1 Earth: Depth versus Temperature	
Depth (km)	Estimated Temperature (°C)
25	20
50	500
100	900

Get the Facts

1. A *seismograph* is an instrument that measures earthquake vibrations called *seismic waves*. The differences in the measurements

EARTH: DEPTH vs. TEMPERATURE

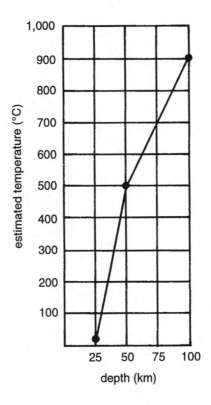

Figure 10.2

of seismic waves coming from different depths allow scientists to indirectly learn about the chemical composition of the interior of the Earth. Find out more about seismographs and how scientists use them to study the inner layers of the Earth.

2. The layers of the Earth have different densities. *Density* is a comparison of the heaviness of a specific amount of material. Find out more about the density of the Earth. What effect do temperature and pressure have on the density of each layer of the Earth? Which layer is most dense? least dense?

The Earth's Lithosphere

Part Four

The Earth's
Lithosphere

Minerals: Distinguishing Physical Characteristics of Minerals

11

The Earth's lithosphere consists of the crust and the upper mantle. The lithosphere is made up mostly of minerals, which are naturally occurring inorganic solids with a definite chemical composition and physical characteristics.

In this project, you will learn a method to determine the specific gravity of a mineral and discover how heft can be used as a method of mineral identification. The difference between cleavage and fracture will be demonstrated. You will use minerals and everyday objects to demonstrate the hardness of minerals. You will learn how to test minerals for their streak and luster. All of this will then be used to prepare a display of minerals that represents their characteristics.

Getting Started

Purpose: To determine the specific gravity of a mineral.

Materials

2-quart (2-liter) bowl

tap water

24-inch (60-cm) piece of string

fist-size sample of quartz, or any any mineral of comparable size

metric spring scale

Procedure

1. Fill the bowl about three-fourths full with water.
2. Tie the string around the mineral and make a loop in the free end of the string.
3. Place the loop on the scale hook and measure the mass of the mineral in grams (see Figure 11.1A). Record this as mass 1 (M_1).

A B

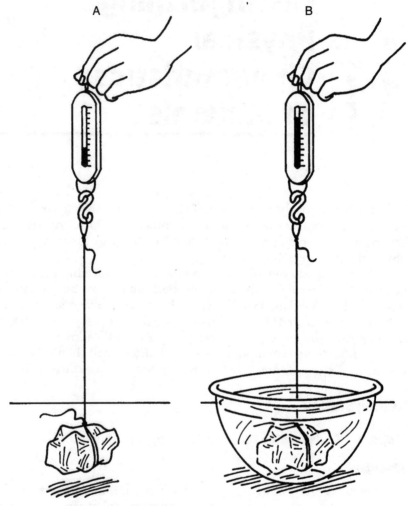

Figure 11.1 A & B

4. With the mineral hanging from the scale, lower the mineral into the water in the bowl (see Figure 11.1B). Do not allow the mineral to rest on the bottom or sides of the bowl. Record this as mass 2 (M_2).

5. Determine the mass of the water **displaced** (pushed out of the way) by the mineral by calculating the absolute difference between M_1 and M_2. Record the answer as mass 3 (M_3).

Example:

$$M_3 = M_1 - M_2$$
$$= 530 \text{ g} - 330 \text{ g}$$
$$= 200 \text{ g}$$

6. Use the following example to determine the mineral's **specific gravity (sp. gr.)**, the ratio of the mass of the mineral in air to the mass of the water displaced by the mineral:

Example:

$$\text{sp. gr.} = M_1 \div M_3$$
$$= 530 \text{ g} \div 200 \text{ g}$$
$$= 2.65$$

Results

A method for determining the specific gravity of a mineral is used. The specific gravity of the mineral in the example is 2.65.

Why?

Most of the elements in the Earth's crust occur as minerals. A mineral is a single solid element or compound found in the Earth and has four basic characteristics: (1) it occurs naturally; (2) it is **inorganic** (not made from living things); (3) it has a definite chemical composition, meaning that it contains the same elements or compounds in the same proportions; and (4) it has a crystalline structure (atoms are arranged so that they form a particular geometric shape).

One way to distinguish one mineral from another is by the specific gravities of the two minerals. To calculate the specific gravity of a mineral, divide the mass of the mineral by the mass of the water displaced by the mineral. Specific gravity tells how many times heavier the mineral is than water. The mineral in the example is 2.65 times as heavy as the same volume of water. Most minerals have a specific gravity from 2 to 5. Since every mineral has a certain specific gravity, this characteristic can be used as a clue to the identity of a mineral.

Specific gravity is not always calculated with a scale. Instead, the heft of minerals is often used in identification. **Heft** is a subjective measurement. You measure heft by picking up minerals of equal volume and comparing their weights. Gold and pyrite are minerals that look alike, but the specific gravity of gold is 19.3 and the specific gravity of pyrite is 5.0. Thus, even though heft is not an exact measurement, the heft of gold is easily determined to be greater than that of pyrite.

Try New Approaches

Would the size of a mineral sample affect its specific gravity measurement? Repeat the experiment two times. First, use a larger piece of quartz; second, use a smaller sample of the mineral. **Science Fair Hint:** Use the mineral samples and their calculated specific gravities as part of a project display.

Design Your Own Experiment

1. **Cleavage** is the property of a mineral when it breaks along a flat surface called a **cleavage plane**. Minerals that break easily and cleanly are described as perfect. Less-clean breaks are described as distinct, indistinct, or none. Minerals can have cleavage in many different directions. Cleavage in one direction is called **basal cleavage**. Muscovite, the most common form of mica, is a mineral that has perfect basal cleavage. Examine a piece of muscovite. You should be able to peel the layers off with your fingers.

   Remove a thin layer of mica and break it in half. Observe the broken edges. This is a **fracture** (an irregular break, one that is not along a cleavage plane). Fracture surfaces are described as uneven, **conchoidal** (curved), **hackly** (jagged), or **splintery** (small, thin, and sharp or fibrous). Use a rock and mineral handbook to identify the type of fracture that muscovite has.

   Collect and display minerals having different types of cleavage and fractures. Use the handbook to find out more about how minerals break and to discover the identity of the cleavage and fracture type for each mineral specimen.

2a. The **hardness** of a mineral is its resistance to being scratched. The scale of hardness from 1 to 10 was devised in 1822 by Frederick Mohs (1773–1839), a German chemist. He arranged 10 common minerals from the softest to the hardest, giving the softest mineral, talc, the number 1, and the hardest mineral, diamond, the number 10. Minerals with higher Mohs' numbers will scratch those with lower numbers. Determine which has a higher Mohs' number, muscovite or quartz. First try to scratch the quartz with the muscovite. Then, try to scratch the muscovite with the quartz. Find the list of minerals for Mohs' scale of hard-

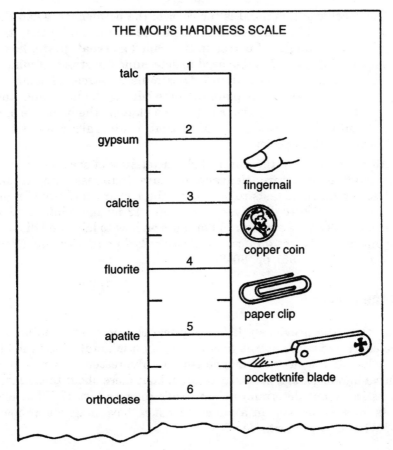

Figure 11.2

ness in a rock and mineral handbook. Prepare a display showing specimens and/or pictures of the minerals for each Mohs' number.

b. Everyday objects such as the following can be used to represent minerals' hardness:

fingernail	2½	glass	6
copper coin (penny)	3½	sandpaper	7
paper clip	4½	steel file	7½
pocket knife blade	5½		

Make and display a chart of the Mohs' scale, similar to the one shown in Figure 11.2.

3. The **streak** of a mineral is the color of the powder left when the mineral is rubbed against a rough surface that is harder than the mineral. An unglazed porcelain tile, called a **streak plate**, has a hardness of about 7 and is used to determine the streak of minerals with a hardness less than 7. Determine the streak of hematite by trying to scratch the plate with the edge of the hematite. Rub your finger over the powder left on the plate by the hematite and determine its streak color. Note that a mineral's color is not always its streak color.

4. All minerals have the physical characteristics of specific gravity, crystalline structure, cleavage, fracture, hardness, and streak. Use the previous tests to determine these characteristics of minerals you wish to display. (See Chapter 12 for more information about crystalline structure.) For hints on how to label and display your minerals, see *Janice VanCleave's Rocks and Minerals* (New York: Wiley, 1996), pp. 80–83.

Get the Facts

Other than the previously listed physical characteristics, minerals have characteristics such as *luster* (the way a mineral reflects light) and color, and some have magnetism and fluorescence. A rock and mineral handbook is a good source to find out more about these characteristics. What determines a mineral's color or luster? What elements must be present in a mineral for it to have magnetic properties? What is phosphorescence?

12

Crystals: Distinguishing Physical Characteristics of Crystals

Minerals have a particular crystalline structure. The shape of the mineral crystal is the same no matter how large the crystal is.

In this project, you will study the six basic crystal shapes, called crystal systems, and show their axes' length and orientation. You will build paper models of the six crystal systems. You will also grow crystals in a solution.

Getting Started

Purpose: To model the axis orientation of a cubic crystal.

Materials

sheet of typing paper
scissors
ruler

three drinking straw of different colors
lemon-size piece of modeling clay

Procedure

1. Cut three 1-inch (2.5-cm) pieces from each of the three colored straws.

2. Divide the clay to form two balls of clay, one to form a walnut-size holder and the other to form a support stand.

3. Insert six straw pieces, two of each color, into the clay holder at 90° to each other, as shown in Figure 12.1. Letters A, B, and C represent the three axes: A, *x*-axis; B, *y*-axis; and C, *z*-axis. Use the remaining three straw pieces to form a legend on the sheet of paper. (An **axis** is a line about which a three-dimensional structure is symmetrical.)

4. Set the clay support stand on the paper.

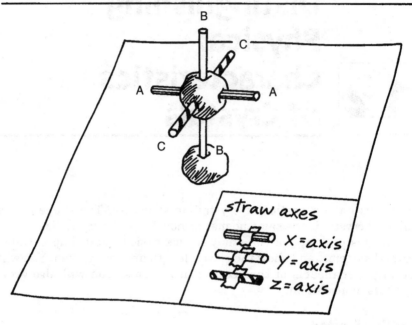

Figure 12.1

Results

A model showing the **axis orientation** (the directional position of the axis of an object) of a cubic crystal is made.

Why?

The Earth's crust contains many kinds of minerals that are identified as one of six crystal systems based on the orientation of their axes. A **crystal** is a solid made up of atoms arranged in an orderly, regular pattern, forming flat **faces** (sides). It has a recognizable shape that results from the repetition of the same combination of atomic particles. The shapes of the crystals in minerals are classified into six different groups called **crystal systems**. There are six common crystal systems: cubic, tetragonal, hexagonal, orthorhombic, monoclinic, and triclinic. All crystals are **three-dimensional**, meaning they have length, width, and depth. In this experiment, a model of a cubic crystal is made. Cubic crystals have three axes that are the same length and at 90° to each other.

Try New Approaches

1a. A tetragonal crystal system has two axes of equal length and one unequal axis. All three of the axes are at 90° to each other. Use the steps of the previous experiment to make a model for a tetragonal crystal. Make the vertical *y*-axis longer or shorter than the other two axes.

b. Make models for the four remaining crystal systems. For information about the length and orientation of the axes of these systems, see the National Audubon Society's *Familiar Rocks and Minerals of North America* (New York: Knopf, 1995), pp. 11–15.

Design Your Own Experiment

A **solution** is a mixture of two or more substances whose makeup is the same throughout. The substance in a solution that dissolves another substance is called the **solvent**. The substance in a solution that is dissolved is called the **solute**. A **saturated solution** is one in which the solvent has dissolved the maximum amount of solute at a given temperature. As the solvent evaporates from a saturated solution, the molecules of excess solute will **precipitate** (separate in solid form from a solution). Crystals can be grown by preparing a surface for the precipitate to stick to. Do this by mixing 1½ cups (375 ml) of epsom salt and 3 cups (750 ml) of water in a 1-quart (1-liter) jar. Coil a 12-inch (30-cm) pipe cleaner around a pencil. Slip the pipe cleaner off the pencil and wrap one end around the middle of the pencil. Suspend the coiled pipe cleaner into the epsom salt solution, as shown in Figure 12.2, so that the pipe cleaner is about ½ inch (1.25 cm) shorter than the depth of the jar.

When the pipe cleaner is soaked with the solution, remove it, lay it on a piece of waxed paper, and let it dry for two or three days. (Keep the jar sealed with a lid during this time.) As the water evaporates from the pipe cleaner, small crystals of epsom salt will cover the surface of the pipe cleaner. Lower the prepared pipe cleaner into the solution and place the uncovered jar where it will be undisturbed at room temperature. Observe the surface of the pipe cleaner periodically for six or more weeks. The tiny crystals on the pipe cleaner provide a surface for the epsom salt precipitates (solids separated from a solution) to stick to, and thus grow into large crystals. If crystals form on the bottom of the jar, carefully lift the pipe cleaner out of the jar and stir to redissolve the precipitated crystals. For more information about crystal growth, see *Janice VanCleave's A+ Projects in Chemistry* (New York: Wiley, 1993), pp. 117–122.

Figure 12.2

Get the Facts

1. A diamond is classed as a gemstone, but graphite isn't. Find out more about the formation of mineral crystals. What are the characteristics of a gemstone? What are crystal twins? See Martyn Bramwell, *Understanding and Collecting Rocks and Fossils* (London: Usborne, 1983), pp. 20–21.

2. Silica is made of silicon and oxygen. It is the most common chemical found in the Earth's crust. The mineral quartz is made of pure silica. Silicates, the largest class of minerals, are composed of metals combined with silica. Find out about silicates. What is the composition of ore minerals? Are silicates considered ore minerals? For information about silicates and other types of minerals, see Dougal Dixon, *The Practical Geologist* (New York: Fireside, 1992), p. 20.

3. A mineral's *habit* refers to its preferred mode of growth, which means the arrangement and proportion of the faces on a single crystal. Find out more about mineral habits in *The Audubon Society Field Guide to North American Rocks and Minerals* (New York: Knopf, 1979), pp. 37–39.

The Rock Cycle: Processes That Change One Rock Type into Another

13

Volcanic rocks and fire rocks are common names for igneous rocks. These solidified masses are, as their names imply, the results of great temperatures within the Earth. Igneous rock is one of a trio of rock types—sedimentary, metamorphic, and igneous. Through different processes, each rock type can be changed into one of the other types in the trio. This process of change is called the rock cycle.

In this project, you will study and model the texture of different igneous rocks. The metamorphism of porphyritic rock (a kind of igneous rock) into foliated metamorphic rock will be demonstrated. You will also examine the relation between the three rock types and model their transformation from one type to the other.

Getting Started

Purpose: To model the difference between a porphyritic rock and other types of igneous rocks.

Materials

two walnut-size pieces of blue modeling clay

two walnut-size pieces of red modeling clay

Procedure

1. Break one red clay piece into four relatively equal size pieces.

2. Roll the four small pieces into balls.

3. Repeat steps 1 and 2 with one blue clay piece.

4. Lay the eight small balls in two rows next to each other, alternating the colors of the balls in the rows.

5. Gently press the clay balls just enough so that they stick together but retain as much of their shape as possible.

Figure 13.1

6. Break the other large red clay piece in half. From one half, form two relatively equal size balls, and from the other half form four relatively equal size balls.

7. Repeat step 6 with the remaining large blue clay piece.

8. Lay the twelve small balls in two rows next to each other, alternating the colors (and sizes) in the rows.

9. Repeat step 5.

10. Compare the appearance of the two clay rolls (see Figure 13.1).

Results

One of the clay rolls has large balls of clay pressed together. The second has large and small balls.

Why?

Rock is a firm, coherent aggregate of one or more minerals. Rocks produced by the cooling and solidifying of molten rock are called **igneous rocks**. **Magma** (molten rock under the Earth's surface) at great depths cools slowly, and during this cooling process, large mineral crystals form. Igneous rocks that form within the crust and contain large uniform interlocking crystals are called **intrusive igneous rocks**. The **texture** of rocks is determined by the size of the mineral **grain** (hard particles) making up the rock. Intrusive igneous rocks are **coarse-grained** (having large hard particles). In this experiment, the clay roll made with large clay balls represents a coarse-grained intrusive igneous rock.

In **porphyritic** rock, like other types of intrusive igneous rock, large crystals form from magma cooling at great depths beneath the Earth's surface. However, during the formation of this rock, the magma is pushed to the surface before it completely hardens. There the final cooling occurs rapidly, producing small crystals. Thus, porphyritic rock contains two or more different sizes of interlocking crystals and can be said to have varied grain sizes. The clay roll with the large and small clay balls represents a porphyritic rock.

Try New Approaches

Lava (molten rock from within the Earth that reaches the Earth's surface) cools quickly, producing rocks with small crystals or no crystals. Igneous rocks formed by the cooling of lava are called **extrusive igneous rocks**. Extrusive rocks are **fine-grained** (having very small hard particles) or have a glassy (smooth) texture. Repeat the experiment using only small balls of clay.

Design Your Own Experiment

1. **Metamorphism** is the change in structure, appearance, and composition of a rock in the solid state within the Earth's crust as a result of changes in temperature and/or pressure. **Regional metamorphism** occurs when large areas of rock are changed by pressure and heat, such as in mountain building. What happens to grain arrangement during regional metamorphism when pressure is applied from one direction? Place a piece of paper on a table and position one of the clay rolls from the original experiment on the paper. Cover the clay with a second sheet of paper. Place a rolling pin on the top paper above one end of the clay roll. Pressing down firmly, roll the rolling pin across the clay roll. Repeat using the second clay roll.

   In nature, great pressure on rocks causes the temperature to rise. Together, the heat and pressure changes cause metamorphism, which produces **metamorphic rock**. Pressing the clay models of igneous rock represents the formation of **foliated metamorphic rock** (striped-looking metamorphic rock with grains arranged in parallel bands). **Science Fair Hint:** Make a display to show the clay rolls before pressure was applied to rep-

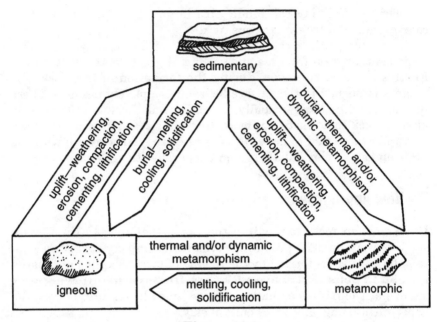

Figure 13.2

resent igneous rock and after pressure was applied in one direction to represent the resulting foliated metamorphic rock.

2a. Rocks come from other rocks. Igneous rock forms when sedimentary or metamorphic rock melts, cools, and solidifies. **Sedimentary rock** is made from **sediments** (materials deposited by water, wind, or glaciers) of metamorphic or igneous rocks that are **compacted** (packed together) and **cemented** (stuck together). Metamorphic rock forms when igneous or sedimentary rock is changed by metamorphism. This never-ending process by which rocks change from one type to another by a series of processes involving heat, pressure, melting, cooling, and sedimentation is called the **rock cycle**. Draw and display a diagram similar to the one shown in Figure 13.2 to represent the rock cycle. Note that sedimentary rocks are placed at the top of the diagram because these rocks are formed when the other rocks are lifted to or near the top of the Earth's surface, while the formation of metamorphic and igneous rocks is generally below the Earth's surface.

b. Use rock samples to prepare a display representing the rock cycle. Use found rocks or rocks purchased at rock and mineral shops or ordered from science catalogs. See Appendix 1 for a list of catalog suppliers and stores selling rocks and minerals.

Get the Facts

Thermal metamorphism includes changes due to heat. *Recrystallization* (enlargement of minerals) is one example of thermal metamorphism. Another example is *contact metamorphism,* which occurs when hot magma intrudes (penetrates into) the rock with which it comes in contact. How large an area is affected by contact metamorphism? What is a metasomatic change? How do contact and regional metamorphism compare? What are the names of different rocks before and after these metamorphic changes? To find out more about metamorphism, see John Farndon, *How the Earth Works* (New York: Reader's Digest Association, 1992), p. 83.

Erosion: The Breakdown and Movement of Crustal Material

14

The physical nature of the Earth's crust is in a constant state of change. The changes are the result of erosion, the process by which the crustal material is broken down and carried away by wind, water, ice, and gravity acting against crustal material.

In this project, you will demonstrate erosion and weathering, the part of erosion that involves only material breakdown. The effects of surface area, composition of materials, humidity, oxidation, and temperature on weathering will be determined. You will also learn about the effect of agents of erosion, such as gravity and water.

Getting Started

Purpose: To demonstrate erosion by water.

Materials

½ cup (125 ml) of soil or coarse sand

four 12-ounce (360-ml) Styrofoam cups

tap water

spoon

cookie sheet

pencil

ruler

masking tape

Procedure

1. Pour the soil into one of the cups, dampen with enough water to make thick mud, and stir.

2. With your hands, mold the mud into eight equal-sized balls.

3. Place the mud balls on the cookie sheet and either allow them to air-dry (which may take three or more days) or, with adult permission, bake them in an oven at 275°F (135°C) for 1 hour or until they are dry.

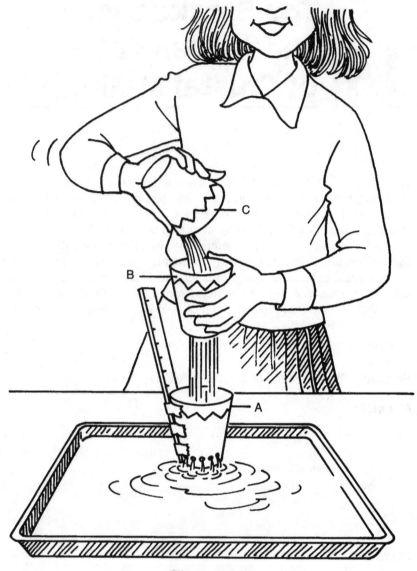

Figure 14.1

4. Prepare the remaining three cups, to be called cups A, B, and C, as follows:

   ■ Use the pencil to make 8 to 10 holes around the bottom edge of cup A.

- Use the pencil to make 12 holes in the bottom of cup B.
- Fill cup C with tap water.
5. Place the dry mud balls in cup A. Observe the shape of the mud balls in the cup.
6. Set cup A in the center of the cookie sheet.
7. Stand the ruler against the side of cup A and secure it to the cup with tape.
8. Hold cup B 4 inches (10 cm) above cup A.
9. Pour the water from cup C into cup B (see Figure 14.1).
10. After the water has drained out of cup B, observe (1) the shape of the mud balls in the cup, and (2) the contents of the cookie sheet.

Results

The mud balls change shape. Parts of the balls are dissolved in the water, and parts are broken off. The dissolved and broken parts are washed out through the holes in the bottom of cup A, where the soil collects on the cookie sheet.

Why?

The mud balls are said to have eroded. **Erosion** is the process by which rock and other materials of the Earth's crust are broken down and carried away by natural agents, such as water, wind, ice, and gravity. The part of erosion that involves only the breakdown of crustal materials is called **weathering**. The crustal materials are broken into pieces by two weathering processes: **chemical weathering**, which affects the chemical properties of substances making up crustal materials, and **mechanical weathering**, which breaks the crustal materials by physical means. Chemical weathering is a **chemical change**, meaning the change produces one or more kinds of matter that are different from those present before the change. Mechanical weathering is a **physical change**, meaning the appearance of matter changes but its properties and makeup remain the same.

This experiment demonstrates one of the main causes of chemical weathering, the action of water. This part of the erosion process is the dissolving of some of the substances forming a solution. Another part is the mixing of the substances with the water forming a **suspension** (a mixture made of parts that separate upon standing). A suspension forms when substances mix with the water but do not dissolve. The water erodes the mud ball by first dissolving and mixing with the substances in the ball, then carrying the substances away.

The agents of erosion in this experiment are water and gravity. Gravity pulls the water down, and the water carries the dissolved materials and mixed substances down with it as it flows out of the holes in the cup. When the water stops moving, gravity pulls the undissolved materials in the water down, where they collect on the pan. Gravity pulls weathered particles to low places. Particles carried away by erosion are called sediments. The buildup of sediments is called **deposition**. Erosion is a wearing-down process, and deposition is a building-up process.

Try New Approaches

1. How does the amount of surface area affect the rate of weathering? Repeat the experiment making 16 equal-sized mud balls. Compare the changes in the shape of the mud balls and the amount of sediment on the cookie sheet in this and the original experiment. More changes in shape and more sediment indicate a faster rate of weathering.

2. How does the composition of material affect its rate of weathering? Repeat the original experiment mixing ¼ cup (63 ml) of soil with ¼ cup (63 ml) of aquarium gravel. **Science Fair Hint:** Display pictures of areas such as Bryce Canyon in Utah and the Grand Canyon in Arizona that show the results of weathering when rocks of different composition, and hence different resistance to weathering, are in the same place.

Design Your Own Experiment

1. One way that mechanical weathering occurs is when water freezes inside cracks in rock. The water expands and may push hard enough to split the rock. Design a way to show how the expansion of freezing water cracks materials. Try mixing water with ½ cup (125 ml) of soil to make eight equal-size mud balls. Put four of the balls on a saucer and place them in a freezer. Put the remaining balls in a second saucer and set them in a warm, dry place. After 24 hours, observe the surface of the two sets of mud balls for cracks. Did the frozen mud balls crack? If not, why? Take photographs of the mud balls at the start and end of the experiment to represent the results. Find out more about other

examples of mechanical weathering. Use the mud ball photographs, photographs from experiments you design, and pictures from books to prepare a display poster representing different types of mechanical weathering.

2a. Rusting is a type of chemical weathering called **oxidation** (combination with oxygen). Rusting is the combination of iron with oxygen in the air to form iron oxide, or rust. Rust is not as strong as iron. Rocks containing iron erode as the iron rusts and the rust crumbles because of gravity, or is moved by water, wind, or ice. Demonstrate oxidation of iron by moistening a lemon-size piece of steel wool with water. *Note:* Use steel wool without soap, available where paint is sold. Wear gloves when handling the steel wool to prevent it from cutting your skin.

In your gloved hand, rub the wet steel wool between your fingers. Observe the firmness of the steel wool. Place the wet steel wool on a saucer and observe its surface for three to five days for signs of rust. When all or most of the surface appears a reddish brown, pick up the rusted steel wool in your gloved hand and again rub it between your fingers. Compare the firmness of the steel wool before and after it rusts.

b. If water is present, rusting occurs quickly and the brown rust limonite is formed. With oxygen alone, the red rust hematite is formed. How does the speed of rusting in high humidity compare with its speed in the presence of water? **Humidity** is the amount of **water vapor** (water in the gas phase) contained in air. Use two identical containers, one for high humidity and the other for low humidity, such as plastic see-through boxes with lids. Cover the bottom of one with a thin layer of water and the bottom of the other with borax, which makes the air dry. Place a bowl in each box and relatively equal size balls of dry steel wool in each bowl (see Figure 14.2). Observe for signs of rust for seven or more days.

Get the Facts

1. After rocks on a hill are weathered, the particles are pulled downhill by gravity. The particles fall or slide and come to rest at the steepest angle at which they can remain stable. This is called the *angle of rest,* or *angle of repose.* Find out more about gravity as an agent of erosion. How does friction affect the angle of rest? See

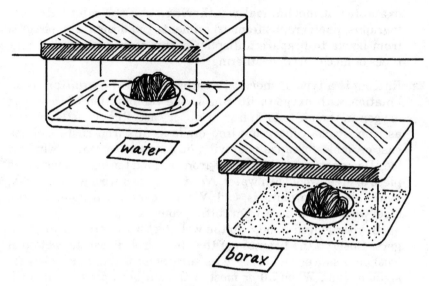

Figure 14.2

John Farndon, *How the Earth Works* (New York: Reader's Digest Association, 1992), p. 108.

2. Ocean waves erode the rocky projections of land that extend into deep water, called *headlands*. Find out more about the erosion of headlands by ocean waves. What is the difference between sea cliffs, sea caves, sea arches, and sea stacks? For information about the erosion of shorelines by wave action, see *Janice VanCleave's Oceans for Every Kid* (New York: Wiley, 1996), pp. 87–94.

15 Rock Sandwiches: Layering of Regolith Particles

Sedimentary rocks are formed from fragments of weathered rocks. The fragments from these rocks that are carried from one place to another by wind, water, ice, and gravity are called sediments. Over millions of years, thick layers of sediments have collected, and their weight has contributed to the compression of the sediments into sedimentary rocks.

In this project, you will demonstrate the formation of sediment layers in sedimentary rock. Lithification, which involves processes that change sediments into clastic rock, are studied and modeled. You will use models to distinguish between the rock fragments making up conglomerate and breccia. You will also demonstrate the formation of the evaporite halite, a chemical sedimentary rock.

Getting Started

Purpose: To demonstrate how horizontal layering can occur in sedimentary rocks.

Materials

scissors
ruler
2-liter plastic soda bottle
2 cups (500 ml) of tap water

1-quart (1-liter) jar with lid
½ cup (125 ml) each of flour, dry rice, and dry red beans (pinto beans work well)

Procedure

1. Cut away the top 4 inches (10 cm) of the soda bottle. Keep the bottom section and discard the top.

2. Pour 1 cup (250 ml) of water into the bottom of the bottle.

3. Put the remaining 1 cup (250 ml) of water into the jar, then add the flour, rice, and beans. Secure the lid and shake to thoroughly mix the materials.

4. Pour the contents of the jar into the bottle.

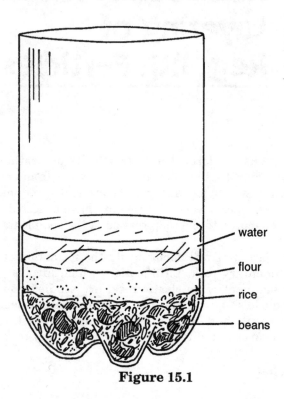

Figure 15.1

5. Observe the initial appearance of the contents of the bottle, then make observations every 20 minutes for 1 hour and again in 24 hours (see Figure 15.1). *Note:* Keep the bottle for the following experiment.

Results

Initially the contents appear cloudy, with beans and rice mixed together in a layer on the bottom. With time, the flour settles, filling the spaces between the beans and rice in the bottom layer and forms a separate top layer.

Why?

The lithosphere is composed mainly of rock and **regolith** (the loose, uncemented rock particles, including soil, that cover the Earth.) Regolith that has been transported by agents of erosion and deposited in another place is called sediment.

The stirring and pouring of the water, flour, rice, and beans mixture into the bottle of water represents the transport of different-size sediments by fast-moving water into a stationary body of water. Sediments, like the food particles in this experiment, settle in stationary water. The settling of the food particles represents the formation of two distinct horizontal sediment layers. The time it takes a sediment to settle out of its transporting agent is called its **settling rate**. The settling rate of the rice and beans is faster than that of the flour. Thus, a lower layer of rice and beans forms first, then the flour fills in the spaces between the rice and beans, and forms a layer above the rice and beans layer.

Try New Approaches

What effect would the addition of more sediments have? Repeat the experiment adding a second mixture of water, flour, rice, and beans after 24 hours. **Science Fair Hint:** Take photographs of the bottle in both experiments and display them to represent the results.

Design Your Own Experiment

1a. **Lithification** is the process, including compaction and cementation, by which newly deposited sediment is converted to sedimentary rock. Lithification of **clasts** (loose fragments made up of bits of older rocks) forms a category of sedimentary rock called **clastic rock**. Lithification of clasts that are 0.08 inch (0.2 cm) in diameter or larger with smooth, rounded edges forms clastic rock called **conglomerate**. Make a model of conglomerate by mixing ¼ cup (63 ml) of plaster of paris with ¼ cup (63 ml) of smooth pebbles in a 9-ounce (270-ml) paper cup. Add enough water to barely cover the mixture. Use a spoon to press down on the surface of the mixture to compact it as much as possible. Allow the cup to sit overnight, then peel away the paper.

b. Lithification of clasts with a diameter of 0.08 inch (0.2 cm) or larger that are angular with rough edges forms clastic rock called **breccia**. Repeat the previous experiment, replacing the smooth pebbles with aquarium gravel. Display the models from this and the previous experiment (see Figure 15.2).

2. **Chemical sedimentary rock** is formed when precipitates of minerals come out of solution and crystallize. Most of these chemical rocks are formed by evaporation of water from a solution and

Figure 15.2

are called **evaporites**. Demonstrate the formation of the evaporite halite (rock salt) by mixing 1 tablespoon (15 ml) of table salt with 2 tablespoons (30 ml) of tap water in a cup. Stir until as much of the salt as possible dissolves. Allow the solution to sit for 2 to 3 minutes. Cover the bottom of a saucer with a circle of black construction paper. Pour the liquid into the saucer. Do not pour the undissolved salt into the saucer. Place the saucer in a warm, dry area. Observe and record the contents of the saucer until all of the water has evaporated. Depending on humidity, this will take 2 to 3 days. Observe the top and bottom of the paper. Find out about other types of evaporites. Prepare a display of evaporites and include the rock salt you made.

Get the Facts

1. Clastic rocks are classified on the basis of particle size. The four basic classes are conglomerate/breccia, sandstone, siltstone, and shale. Find out more about clastic sedimentary rocks. What are the ranges of clast sizes in each of the four classes? What are the differences between quartz, arkosic, and lithic sandstone? What is the difference between lithification and diagenesis? For information about clastic rocks, see Brian J. Skinner and Stephen C. Porter, *The Dynamic Earth* (New York: Wiley, 1992), pp. 118–119 and 120–125.

2. Rocks containing a large number of *ooids,* often referred to as *ooliths,* are called *oolites.* Find out more about this type of rock. What is the shape, size, and composition of ooliths? Under what conditions do they form? For information about oolites, see Pat Bell and David Wright, *Rocks and Minerals* (New York: Macmillan, 1986), p. 134.

3. The three classifications of sedimentary rocks are clastic, chemical, and organic. *Organic rocks* are formed from living things or their remains. Find out more about organic rocks.

16 Soil Texture: Effects of Regolith Size

A great part of the Earth's crust is covered with plant growth. The survival of these plants depends on the physical and nutritional support they receive from a mixture of particles of weathered rock and humus called soil.

In this project, you will learn the differences between coarse-, medium-, and fine-textured soils. How the texture of soil and the shape of its particles affects a soil's porosity will be determined. You will also examine the relation between soil texture and permeability. Soil profile and types will be studied.

Getting Started

Purpose: To determine the texture of soil.

Materials

garden trowel

1-quart (1-liter) bowl

marker

masking tape

three identical 1-pint
(500-ml) transparent jars

1 quart (1 liter) of soil

newspaper

colander with large holes

large fine-mesh strainer

Procedure

1. Select a spot with soil, such as near a tree or where plants are growing. A bare soil area in a garden is also acceptable. Ask for permission to remove about 1 quart (1 liter) of soil.

2. Use the trowel to fill the bowl with soil.

3. Use the marker and tape to number the jars 1, 2, and 3.

4. Lay the newspaper on a table.

5. Spread the soil on the newspaper and pick out any live animals and parts of dead animals and plants, and return them to where the soil was collected.

Figure 16.1

6. Pour the soil into the colander, and shake the colander over the newspaper until no more particles fall through the holes in the colander (see Figure 16.1).

7. Put the particles left in the colander into jar 1.

8. Pour the particles on the newspaper into the fine-mesh strainer. Shake the strainer over the paper until no particles fall through.

9. Put the particles in the strainer into jar 2 and the particles on the newspaper into jar 3.

10. Compare the amount of material in each jar.

Results

The soil is separated into three sizes of particles—large, medium, and small. The amount of material in each jar will vary with different soil samples.

Why?

Soil is the top layer of the regolith that supports plant growth. Soil is composed of particles from weathered rock, **humus** (decayed animal and plant matter), air, and water. Soil is necessary for life of both plants and animals. It provides the building blocks of materials that most plants need to make food. And animals, either directly or indirectly, depend on plants for food.

All soils are not alike. The weathered rock samples come from different kinds of rocks, and the amount and composition of humus vary. Most soil contains particles of varying size. In this experiment, you separated the particles. Coarse-grained particles, as in jar 1, are larger than **medium-grained** particles, as in jar 2. Fine-grained particles, as in jar 3, are smaller than the other two particle types. The texture of soil depends on which type of particles predominates in the soil. For example, if there are more particles in jar 3, then your soil sample would be considered fine-textured.

Try New Approaches

1a. Soil texture can be estimated by rubbing it between your fingers. Determine the feel of different textures, then collect a variety of soil samples from very coarse to very fine.

b. Compare the amount of the different-size particles in each sample collected in the previous experiment by repeating the original experiment. **Science Fair Hint:** Use photographs or diagrams of the jars of particles to represent the comparison of particles in different soil textures.

Design Your Own Experiment

1. Porosity is the percentage of a material's volume that is **pore space** (small, narrow spaces between particles in materials). How does the shape of soil particles affect porosity? Compare rounded and angular-shaped objects of comparable size. For example, compare smooth rocks or beads with aquarium gravel. Fill a measuring cup with the round objects. Note the visible spaces between the objects. Measure the volume of the spaces by filling the cup to the 1-cup (250 ml) mark with a measured amount of water. Repeat, replacing the rounded objects with the angular-shaped objects. Repeat again, using a mixture of equal parts of the rounded and angular objects.

2. **Permeability** is the measure of how easily water flows through a material. If water flows quickly through soil, the soil is said to have high permeability. How does texture relate to the permeability of soil? Use the point of a pencil to make six equal-size holes in the bottom of three 9-ounce (270 ml) paper cups. Cut circles from coffee filters to fit in the bottom of each cup. Label the cups "coarse," "medium," and "fine." Mark a line 2 inches (5 cm) from the bottom of each cup. Fill to this line with samples of the three soil textures corresponding to the labels on the cups. Lay two pen-

Figure 16.2

Table 16.1 Soil Permeability			
Soil Type	Draining Time	Amount of Water Drained	Drainage Rate
coarse-textured			
medium-textured			
fine-textured			

cils parallel to each other across a plate, then set the cup of coarse sand on the pencils, making sure that the pencils do not cover the holes in the cup (see Figure 16.2). Ask a helper to time you as you pour 100 ml of tap water into the cup. Stop timing when no more water drains from the cup. Record the draining time in a chart like Table 16.1. Measure the amount of water that drained from the cup by pouring the water from the plate into a measuring cup. Record the amount of water in milliliters. Calculate the drainage rate by dividing the amount of water drained by the time it took to drain. Record this answer. Repeat the procedure with the other soil samples. The most permeable soil is the one with the highest drainage rate.

Get the Facts

1. A cutaway section of the Earth would reveal a soil profile made up of layers called *horizons*. Mature soils have three basic horizons. What is the composition of each horizon? For information about horizons, see David Lambert and the Diagram Group, *The Field Guide to Geology* (New York: Facts on File, 1988), p. 106.

2. *Pedologists* (soil scientists) divide soil into different types. Six basic types are tundra, desert, chernozem, ferralsol, brown forest, and red-yellow podzol. What types of plants grow in each soil type? How does climate affect soil types? What is the composition of the different soil types? For information about soil types, see *The Field Guide to Geology,* pp. 108–109.

3. Soils differ in the size of the particles they contain. Soil types in order of decreasing particle size are sand, silt, and clay. Most soils

are not pure sand, silt, or clay, but mixtures of all the types. Such mixtures are called *loam*. How much sand is needed for the soil to be called sandy loam? What is a heavy soil? a light soil? See "soil" in various encyclopedias for information about soil.

Crustal Bending: Deformation of the Earth's Crust

17

Stress acting on rock layers can cause deformation. The results of the past up-and-down and in-and-out movements of the layers are not always apparent from the surface because surface evidence may have worn away over time. Thus, the underlying patterns of deformed layers are often evident only when sections of the Earth are cut away, as with the making of roadways.

In this project, you will demonstrate three types of stress that cause rock deformation—compression, tension, and shear—as well as the different types of deformations that result from each type of stress.

Getting Started

Purpose: To model the formation of an anticline.

Materials

permanent marker

sponge

tap water

Procedure

1. Use the marker to make a line around the perimeter of the sponge through the center of its outside edge.

2. Moisten the sponge with water to make it pliable, then lay it on a table.

3. Without lifting the sponge, place your hands on its short ends and push the ends toward the center of the sponge (see Figure 17.1). Observe the movement and shape of the sponge.

Results

The center of the sponge bends upward in an arch shape.

Why?

The line drawn on the sponge divides the sponge into layers representing **strata** (layers of rock material) in the Earth's crust. The

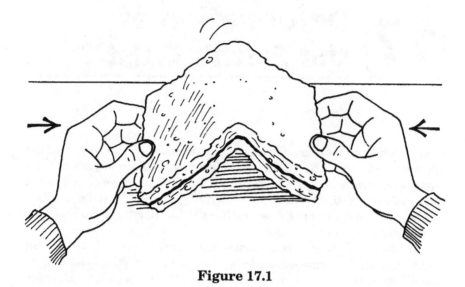

Figure 17.1

force applied to the sponge represents a form of **stress**, which is a force that acts on rocks in the Earth's crust, causing movement or a change in shape or volume. The type of stress represented in this experiment is **compression** (squeezing together) of rock. Compression can cause rock to break or bend. The movement of the sponge demonstrated a **folding**, or bending of rock layers. A fold producing an upward arch shape is called an **anticline**.

Try New Approaches

A **syncline** is a fold that curves down, creating a troughlike shape. Hold the sponge from the experiment and apply a compression force to cause it to fold downward. By tilting your hands a little, you should be able to first form an anticline, then a syncline.

Design Your Own Experiment

1a. Anticlines are not always visible at the surface. They can be eroded or covered with other materials so that the surface is flat instead of bulging upward. A model of a square cut from the Earth can be made to show the folding of the strata beneath the flat surface. Draw a design, such as the one shown in Figure 17.2, on a sheet of typing paper, and color each stratum to indicate dif-

ANTICLINE

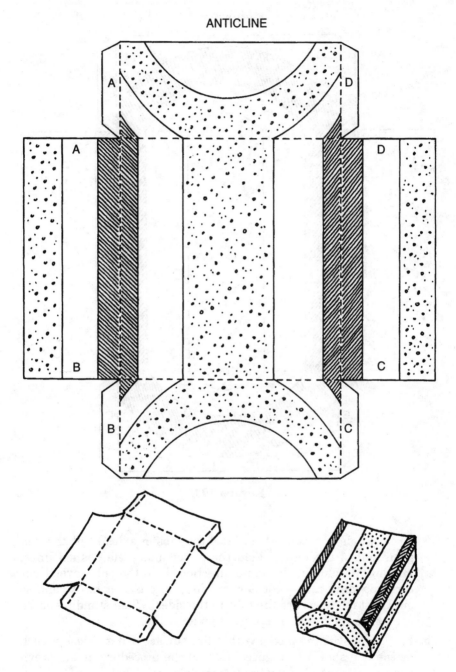

Figure 17.2

SYNCLINE

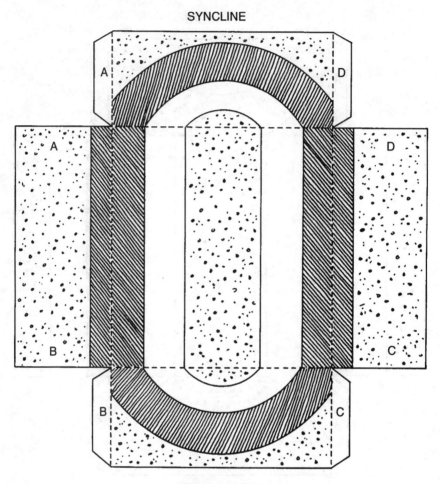

Figure 17.3

ferent kinds of rocks. (Don't label the tabs or sides.) Cut the diagram out of the paper. Fold the paper along the dashed lines, making all folds in the same direction. Fold the sides over their corresponding tabs—side A over tab A, size B over tab B, and so on. Use tape to secure the tabs to the sides. When standing on its open side, the box will represent an anticline.

b. Prepare a syncline model with a flat surface using a design such as the one shown in Figure 17.3 and the procedure in the previous experiment. Display the two models with labels.

Get the Facts

1. A rock placed under increasing stress goes through three stages of deformation in succession: elastic deformation, ductile deformation, and fracture. What is an elastic limit? Which deformations are irreversible changes? For information about the stages of deformation, see Brian J. Skinner and Stephen C. Porter, *The Dynamic Earth* (New York: Wiley, 1995), pp. 410–411.

2. The Himalayas are the biggest fold mountains on Earth. They are also the largest mountains and have the twenty-eight tallest peaks. What are the characteristics of fold mountains? How were the Himalayas and other fold mountains formed? At what rate are the Himalayas growing? What are other examples of fold mountains? Where are fold mountains generally found? Prepare a display map showing the locations and names of fold mountains. For information about fold mountains, see Steve and Jane Parker, *Mountains and Valleys* (San Diego: Thunder Bay Press, 1996), pp. 20–21.

18 Faulting: The Earth's Crustal Breaking Point

Faulting results when the Earth's crust not only breaks but moves. Stress produces motion in different directions and causes the separate pieces to move in relation to each other. The motion of the crust after breaking is used to classify faults.

In this project, you will study and model the different types of faults and the types of stress that cause them. You will also use models to show the Earth's surface features as a result of faulting.

Getting Started

Purpose: To determine the distinguishing characteristics of a normal fault.

Materials

two lemon-size pieces of clay of different colors

table knife

two round toothpicks

Procedure

1. Break each piece of clay in half.
2. Shape each piece of clay into a roll about 4 inches (10 cm) long.
3. Lay the clay rolls together, one on top of the other, alternating the colors.
4. Press the rolls together into one large clay piece. Flatten the sides of the clay piece by tapping them against a hard surface, such as a table.
5. Use the table knife to cut the clay piece into two parts diagonally.
6. Secure the layers in each part together by inserting a toothpick through the layers, top to bottom.
7. Hold the parts together so that the colored layers match up, then move the left part up and the right part down, as shown in Figure 18.1.

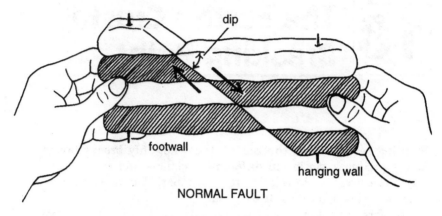

NORMAL FAULT

Figure 18.1

Results

The clay is cut and shifted so that the layers of colored clay in the two parts no longer form continuous horizontal lines.

Why?

Each clay color represents a stratum of one kind of rock material. Cutting the clay represents the stress that causes the Earth's crust to fracture. If there is no movement along the fracture, the fracture is called a **joint**. But if there is movement, the fracture is called a **fault**. The fracture line of a fault is called the **fault plane**. If the fault plane shows vertical displacement (up-and-down movement), the **fault block** (rock that bounds a fault plane) above the fault plane is called the **hanging wall** and the fault block below the fault plane is called the **footwall**. In this experiment, the hanging wall of the fault moves down in relation to the footwall. The stress represented is **tension** (the stretching, or pulling apart, of rocks), and the type of fault modeled is a **normal fault**. The angle formed by the fault plane and the top of the hanging wall, measured from the horizontal, is called the **dip** (see Figure 18.1).

While the hanging wall and footwall of the model both moved, it is not always possible to determine whether two fault blocks of the Earth move or whether one stands still while the other moves past it. Fault types are classified by relative displacement, that is, how one side of a fault is pushed out of place in a given direction relative to the other side. With a normal fault, the hanging wall moves down in relation to the footwall.

Try New Approaches

1. Compression causes a **reverse fault**. This fault is similar to a normal fault, except the hanging wall moves upward in relation to the footwall. Repeat the experiment moving the hanging wall up and the footwall down to model a reverse fault.

2. **Shearing** (stress that twists, tears, or pushes rocks past each other) produces a **lateral fault**, also called a **strike-slip fault**. The movement of a lateral fault along a vertical fault plane is mainly horizontal, with little or no up-and-down movement. The left or right direction is determined by an observer standing on either fault block: the movement of the other block is a **left lateral fault** if it is to the left or a **right lateral fault** if it is to the right. Repeat the original experiment twice, making two clay models. Use one model to represent a right lateral fault and the other a left lateral fault. **Science Fair Hint:** Display the models for each type of fault. Display before-and-after photographs of the position of the clay model representing the different types of faulting.

Design Your Own Experiment

1. A fault block displaced downward and bounded by parallel normal faults is called a **graben** or **rift**. The steep-walled **rift valley** (long, narrow breaks in the Earth's crust) that runs down the center of the mid-Atlantic Ridge is a graben. (For more information about rift valleys in this and other midocean ridges, see Chapter 19, "Plate Tectonics.") An upthrust block bounded by parallel faults is called a **horst**. Use salt dough to make models showing these fault blocks. For each color of dough, mix 2 cups (500 ml) of flour and ½ cup (125 ml) of table salt in a bowl. Add 20 drops of food coloring to ¾ cup (188 ml) of water. Add the colored water to the salt and flour mixture. Knead the dough about 3 minutes or until it is soft and pliable. *Note:* Add a little more flour if the dough feels sticky or a little more water if it feels dry.

   Shape three or more 1 × 1 × 4-inch (2.5 × 2.5 × 10-cm) alternating layers of colored dough on a cookie sheet. Cut two diagonal fault planes for each model. The bottom of the first planes should slant inward with the fault block moved down to represent a graben (see Figure 18.2A). In the second model, the bottom of the planes should slant outward with the fault block moved up to represent a horst (see Figure 18.2B). With adult permission,

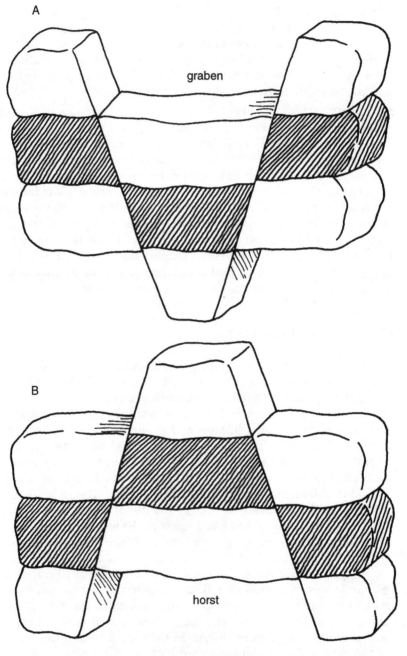

Figure 18.2A & B

bake the dough at 275°F (135°C) for 2 hours or until the dough is firm. For information about fault blocks, see David Lambert and the Diagram Group, *The Field Guide to Geology* (New York: Facts on File, 1988), p. 91.

2a. How does tensional stress affect the width of the crust in a **fault zone** (area of Earth's crust that includes the fault blocks on both sides of the fault plane)? On a 4 × 6-inch (10 × 15-cm) piece of cardboard, draw and label the shapes shown in Figure 18.3, then cut out the shapes. Lay the pieces together on a table so that all their edges are even. Measure and record the total width of the assembled pieces. Demonstrate normal faulting caused by tensional stress by moving the two hanging walls down about 1 inch (2.5 cm). Measure and record the total width of the assembled pieces in this normal faulting position.

b. How does compressional stress affect the width of the crust in a fault zone? Assemble the pieces from the previous experiment to form a 4 × 6-inch (10 × 15-cm) rectangle. Demonstrate reverse faulting caused by compressional stress by moving the two foot-

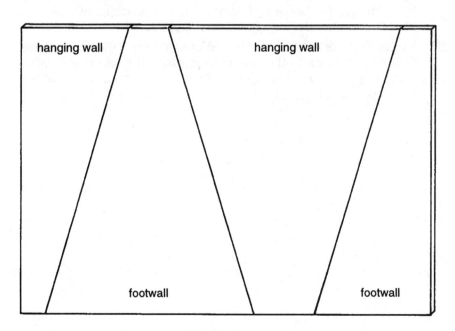

Figure 18.3

walls down about 1 inch (2.5 cm), and push the pieces together. Measure and record the total width of the assembled pieces in this reverse faulting position.

c. How would the dip of the fault plane affect the results of the two previous experiments? Repeat each experiment twice. First, use cardboard pieces with a smaller fault plane dip. Then use cardboard pieces with a larger fault plane dip.

Get the Facts

1. The largest recorded abrupt vertical displacement occurred in 1899 at Yakutat Bay, Alaska. Part of the Alaskan shore was lifted as much as 50 feet (15 m) above sea level. Is movement along fault planes always abrupt? How does the depth of the San Andreas fault affect its movement? For information about movement along fault planes, see Brian J. Skinner and Stephen C. Porter, *The Dynamic Earth* (New York: Wiley, 1995), pp. 414–415.

2. The Grand Tetons of Wyoming are fault block mountains. Find out more about the formation of fault block mountains. What is a thrust fault? See Steve and Jane Parker, *Mountains and Valleys* (San Diego: Thunder Bay Press, 1996), pp. 22–23.

3. Faults that are temporarily locked together are called *lock faults*. How can these and other faults produce earthquakes? For information, see *Janice VanCleave's Earthquakes* (New York: Wiley, 1993), pp. 12–15 and 24–27.

19 Plate Tectonics: Floating Crustal Sections

The Earth's lithosphere is made up of sections called plates that move in relation to each other. This movement is made possible because the plates float on the asthenosphere, which has a thick mudlike texture.

In this project, you will demonstrate seafloor spreading at mid-ocean ridges. You will use models of seafloor spreading to indicate the changes in the Earth's magnetic field over long periods of time. You will learn about the theory of plate tectonics. You will also model the movement of lithospheric plates at divergent boundaries, convergent boundaries, and transform boundaries.

Getting Started

Purpose: To demonstrate seafloor spreading.

Materials

sheet of typing paper

scissors

42-ounce (1.19-kg) empty, round oatmeal box

serrated knife (use with adult approval)

Procedure

1. Fold the paper in half lengthwise with the long edges together.

2. Unfold the paper and cut it in half along the fold line.

3. Use the knife to cut a ¼ × 5-inch (0.63 × 12.5-cm) slit in the side of the box.

4. Put the paper strips together, one on top of the other, then push the papers down through the slit in the box. Keep about 2 inches (5 cm) of the strips on the outside and fold them back on opposite sides of the slit.

5. Hold the ends of the strips, one in each hand, and slowly pull about 6 inches (15 cm) of the papers in opposite directions along the surface of the box (see Figure 19.1).

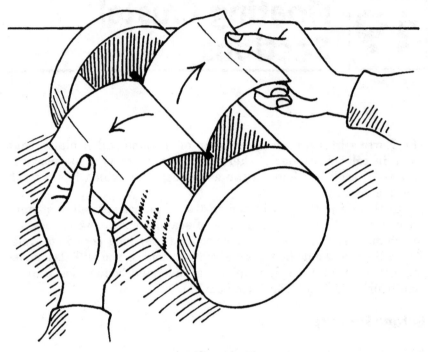

Figure 19.1

Results

The paper strips emerge from the box and move along the box's surface in opposite directions.

Why?

Where the papers exit, the box represents a **midocean ridge** (one of a number of ridges forming a continuous chain of underwater mountains around the Earth). In the center of the midocean ridge is a rift valley. A rift valley is a deep, narrow crack in the Earth's crust, like the slit in the box. Molten rock rises to the surface through this crack. About half of the lava rising out of the rift valley spreads on either side of the midocean ridge. The portion of crust on either side of the ridge is moved apart by the addition of the new material. The lava hardens and forms new ocean floor. This process of the creation of new oceanic crust that moves slowly away from the midocean ridges is called **seafloor spreading**.

Evidence of seafloor spreading is a pattern of parallel magnetic "stripes" that are identical on each side of a midocean ridge. The magnetic stripes came about because, before the lava solidified into rock, the mineral grains of magnetic iron in the lava aligned in the direction of the Earth's **magnetic field** (region in which magnetic materials are acted on by magnetic forces). When the lava solidified, the grains of the rock were permanently fixed in the direction of the Earth's magnetic field. But because the Earth's magnetic field has reversed itself many times over millions of years, stripes of rock next to each other may have grains aligned in different directions.

Try New Approaches

1. Represent the formation of magnetic stripes on the crust beneath the ocean by pulling the paper strips out of the box so that about 2 inches (5 cm) of the paper comes out of the slit on both sides. Use a colored marker to make a colored stripe about ½ inch (1.25 cm) wide across the paper strips where they come out of the box. Pull the paper strips so that another ½ inch (1.25 cm) comes out the slit. Use a different-colored marker to color the new white paper above the slit. Continue to pull out ½ inch (1.25 cm) of new paper from the slit, alternating the colors until six to eight matching stripes are made on each side of the paper. **Science Fair Hint:** Display the model of the magnetic stripes along with a diagram, similar to Figure 19.2, showing a midocean ridge with magnetic stripes on either side of the ridge. Use arrows to indicate the reversed directions of the stripes.

2. While the seafloor may spread from 1 to 5 inches (2.5 to 12.5 cm) or more per year, the total amount of crust stays the same. This is because as new crust is being formed at the midocean ridges, old crust is sinking into the asthenosphere, where it melts and is absorbed into the mantle. Represent this movement by repeating the original experiment, but cut three slits, 4 inches (15 cm) apart, in the box. Tape both strips of paper, one on top of the other, to a pencil, near its point (see Figure 19.3A). Wind all but about 6 inches of the paper around the pencil. Position the box on its side, with the center slit on top and a slit on each side. Place the pencil and paper strips inside the box. Separate the strips, pushing one strip out through each of the side slits. Put the ends of the strips together and push them down through the center slit. From inside the box, pull the papers down as far as possible without pulling the strips off the pencil. Slowly turn the pencil to wrap the paper around it as you observe the movement of the paper on the outside of the box (see Figure 19.3B). For more information

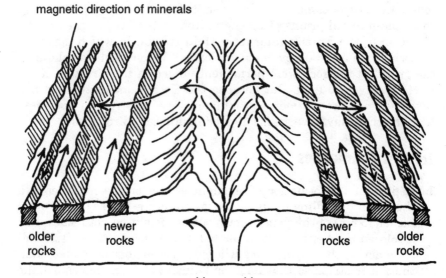

magnetic direction of minerals

older rocks

newer rocks

newer rocks

older rocks

midocean ridge

Figure 19.2

about seafloor spreading, see David Lambert and the Diagram Group, *The Field Guide to Geology* (New York: Facts on File, 1988), pp. 40–43.

Design Your Own Experiment

1. According to the theory of **plate tectonics**, the Earth's lithosphere is divided into sections called **plates**. These plates float on top of the asthenosphere much like flat rocks on thick mud. Use an earth science text to find out about the lithospheric plates. Prepare a display diagram showing the shapes, names, and locations of the plates. For information about plate tectonics, see Thomas R. Watters, *Planets* (New York: Macmillan, 1995), pp. 84–85.

2a. The boundary where lithospheric plates move away from each other, such as at the midocean ridges, is called a **divergent boundary**. Prepare a model of plates at a divergent boundary: Cover a small box with a solid-color paper and label it "Astheno-

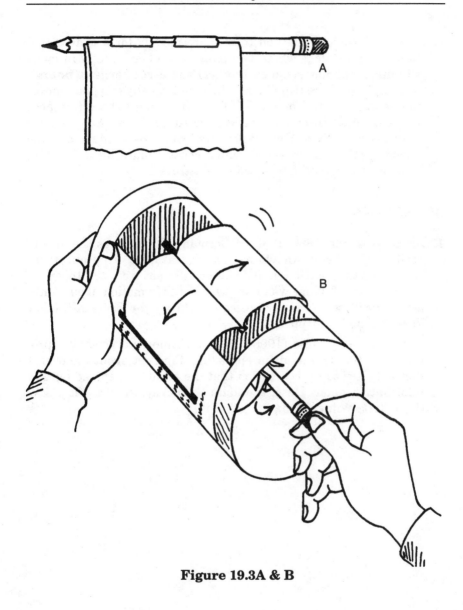

Figure 19.3A & B

sphere." Lay two sponges on top of the box so they are slightly separated. Label each sponge "Plate" and add directional arrows, indicating movement of the plates in opposite horizontal directions. Make a stand-up sign by folding an index card in half lengthwise and labeling the card "Divergent Boundary."

b. Use the previous method to prepare models for a **transform boundary** (a place where two plates slide horizontally in opposite directions alongside each other) and a **convergent boundary** (a place where two plates collide and usually one plate moves under the other). For more information about the differences between these three boundaries, see Keith Stowe, *Essentials of Ocean Science* (New York: Wiley, 1987), pp. 26–35. Make a model showing the boundaries at which crustal material is created, destroyed, and neither created nor destroyed.

Get the Facts

1. Alfred Wegener (1880–1930), a German scientist, was the first to propose the theory known as continental drift. Find out about Wegener's theory. How is it alike or different from the theory of plate tectonics? What was Pangaea? For information about continental drift, see *Janice VanCleave's Oceans for Every Kid* (New York: Wiley, 1996), pp. 5–11.

2. In 1960, Harry Hess (1906–1969), an American geologist, proposed the theory of seafloor spreading. Find out about the events that led Hess to his conclusion that the seafloor is spreading. For information about Hess, see John S. Dickey, Jr., *On the Rocks* (New York: Wiley, 1988), pp. 145–148.

Part Five

The Earth's Hydrosphere

Soundings: Mapping a Profile of the Ocean Floor

20

The first scientific attempt to measure the depth of the ocean was made during an expedition by the ship *Challenger* between 1872 and 1876. The measuring method on the *Challenger* was called sounding and involved lowering weighted ropes to the ocean bottom. Today investigators use echo-sounding sonar and other methods to determine ocean depths.

In this project, you will model the use of sonar to determine ocean depths. You will also determine how to use echo soundings to graph a profile of the ocean floor and learn how distances between echo soundings affect accuracies of profiles.

Getting Started

Purpose: To model the use of sonar to determine ocean depth.

Materials

tennis ball

helper

stopwatch

calculator

Procedure

1. Hold your arms against the side of your body, then bend your elbows at a 90° angle so that your hands are held straight out in front of you.

2. Hold the ball in one hand.

3. Standing still and keeping your elbows against your sides, practice bouncing the ball several times until you can throw it with the least amount of force to cause it to return to your other hand (see Figure 20.1).

4. Ask a helper to measure the time it takes for the ball to leave one hand and return to the other. When your helper says "go" and

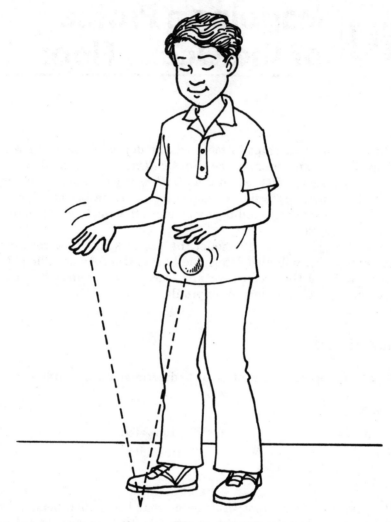

Figure 20.1

starts the stopwatch, throw the ball. When you catch the ball, say "stop" and have your helper stop the watch and record the time that has passed as the echo time.

5. Repeat step 4 three more times and average the results by adding together the four recorded echo times and dividing the sum by 4.

Example:

0.56 sec + 1.02 sec + 0.59 sec + 1.0 sec = 3.17 seconds
3.17 sec ÷ 4 = 0.7925 = 0.79 seconds

6. The depth of the ocean floor (*D*) is one-half the average echo time (*t*) multiplied by the speed of sound in water (*S*). Use the average echo time to model how the depth in water could be determined by the following formula:

$$D = \frac{1}{2}t \times S$$

The speed of sound in ocean water is about 5,000 feet per second (1,500 meters per second), which can be written 5,000 ft/sec (1,500 m/sec).

Example:

$$D = \frac{1}{2} \times 0.79 \text{ sec} \times 5,000 \text{ ft/sec (1,500 m/sec)}$$
$$= 1,975 \text{ feet (592.5 m)}$$

Results

The time for the ball to bounce and return will vary depending on the height of the person throwing it. For the example, the average time was 0.79 seconds. Using this as a model of the sonar echo time in the ocean, the ocean depth was calculated to be 1,975 feet (592.5 m).

Why?

Mapping the ocean floor requires methods different from those used on land. In the past, the depth was measured by a method called **sounding**. Sounding has nothing to do with sound. To take a sounding, knots were tied in a rope at intervals of **1 fathom** (6 feet, or 1.8 m). A weight was tied at one end of the rope and dropped over the side of the ship. The number of knots that went over the side before the weight struck bottom was counted. The number of knots equaled the depth in fathoms.

A modern method of measuring ocean depth is **echo sounding**, which is a method of sending out sound from a transmitter and measuring the **echo time** (time it takes sound leaving a transmitter to

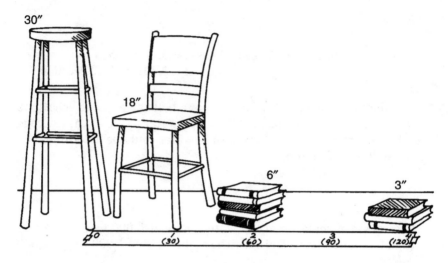

Figure 20.2

travel to an object, be reflected, and return to a receiver). Echo sounding is often called sonar. The term **sonar** stands for *SO*und *N*avigation *A*nd *R*anging. Sonar is a method or device used to determine ocean depth or distance by calculating the echo time of sound.

In this experiment, the bouncing ball represents sound bouncing off the ocean floor. The time for the round trip—the echo time—was measured and used to calculate the one-way distance—the depth.

Try New Approaches

1a. Model measuring the depth of different parts of the ocean floor by taping a 4-foot (120-cm) piece of adding machine tape to a tile floor. Write 0 at one end and mark each foot (30 cm) from 1 foot to 4 feet (30 cm to 120 cm), as shown. Position a stool on the zero mark and a chair at the 1-foot (30-cm) mark, and stack five or six thick books at the 2-foot (60-cm) mark and two or three books at the 4-foot (120-cm) mark (see Figure 20.2). Now, using the stool, the chair, and the books as part of the ocean floor, repeat the original experiment, measuring the echo sound by bouncing the ball at each of the four marks. At zero, the stool that represents the shoreline, record the time as zero, then move to the 1-foot

Table 20.1 Depth of Ocean		
Distance from Shoreline	Average Echo Time	Calculated Depth
0 foot (0 m)	0 second	0 foot (0 m)
1 foot (30 cm)	0.35 second	875 feet (262.5 m)
2 feet (60 cm)	0.52 second	1,300 feet (390 m)
3 feet (90 cm)	0.80 second	2,000 feet (600 m)
4 feet (120 cm)	0.68 second	1,700 feet (510 m)

(30-cm) mark, drop the ball, and time the echo. Continue moving to each mark on the tape, dropping and timing the bouncing ball. Record the measurements in a data table like Table 20.1. Use the depth equation to calculate the depth at each distance from the shoreline, and record it in the data table.

b. Use the calculated depths from the data table to plot a graph representing the profile of the ocean floor (see Figure 20.3).

c. How does the distance between the echo soundings affect the accuracy of the profile? Repeat parts 1a and 1b taking echo soundings every 6 inches from the model's shoreline. Compare the profiles made with 1-foot (30-cm) soundings and 6-inch (15-cm) soundings to determine which better represents a profile of the ocean model.

Design Your Own Experiment

1a. Design another ocean model representing a section of the ocean, and use sounding to map the ocean model's profile. One way is to place two identical chairs, with backs at least 30 inches (70 cm) tall, 4 feet (1.2 m) apart. Represent the surface of the ocean by tying a string horizontally between the highest points of the chairs. Use a black marking pen to mark off 3-inch (7.5-cm) intervals along the "surface" string. Place stacked books, a stool, and an upturned pot and bowl under the string. These objects represent features on the ocean floor.

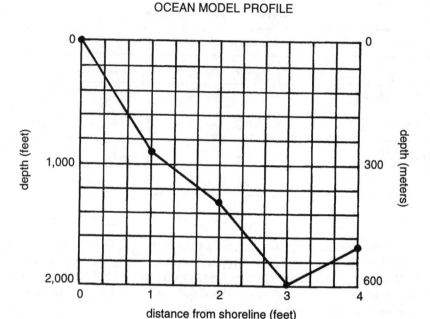

Figure 20.3

Cut a second string 12 inches (30 cm) longer than the height of the chairs. Tie a washer to one end. Use the pen to mark off a 1-inch (2.5-cm) scale along this second string. This string will be called the scale. Holding the free end of the scale, position it against the surface string, next to the back of one chair (this is the 0-inch, or 0-cm, mark) and slowly lower the scale until the washer touches an object or the floor. Use the marks on the scale to determine the depth of the ocean at that point. Round off the measurement to the nearest scale marking. Measure the depth of the ocean every 3 inches (7.5 cm) along the length of the surface string, and record the depth measurements and the distances from the shoreline (the zero mark) in a data table like Table 20.1.

b. Use the data table to make a graph of your measurements. Title the graph "Ocean Model Profile." Display the graph and a photograph of the profile of the ocean model.

Get the Facts

The profile of the ocean floor is divided into four areas: the continental shelf, the continental slope, the continental rise, and the abyss. Which areas make up the *continental margin* (water-covered area from the shoreline of the continents to the abyss)? What is the location and size of each area? For information about these four ocean areas, see Don Groves, *The Oceans* (New York: Wiley, 1989), pp. 96–97. Display a diagram of the ocean profile showing the four areas.

21

Water Waves: Surface Disturbances Due to Energy Transfer

Water waves behave in a similar manner to waves moving through a rope. A rope moves up and down as the waves move forward, but the rope does not move forward with the waves. Similarly, waves pass through water but do not carry the water with them. It is the wave energy that moves forward.

In this project, you will learn about water waves and model their structure and movement. You will use models to distinguish between movement of water molecules and wave energy.

Getting Started

Purpose: To model the parts of a wave.

Materials

scissors

ruler

two 5 × 8-inch (12.5 × 20-cm) index cards

transparent tape

sheet of typing paper

colored, transparent plastic report folder

black marking pen

Procedure

1. Along a long edge of one index card, centered left/right, cut a 3 × 4-inch rectangular U-shaped piece out of the card (discard the piece).

2. Place the cut card on top of the second index card with the cut-out shape at the top.

3. Secure the two cards together with tape only on the long sides (top and bottom). Do not put tape on the cut-out part. These connected cards will serve as the wave viewer.

4. Fold the paper in half, long sides together.

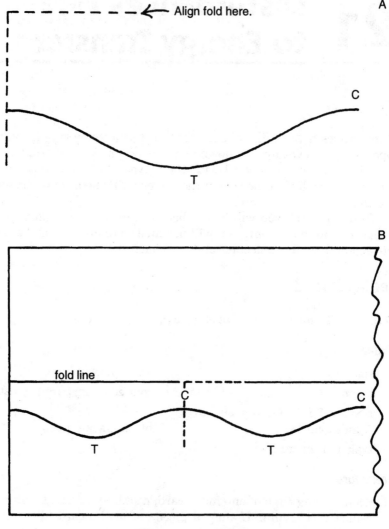

Figure 21.1A & B

5. To make a wave for your viewer, unfold the paper and lay it over the diagram of the wave in Figure 21.1A: match the corner of the paper formed by the fold line and the paper's left side with the corner of the diagram where the dashed lines meet.

6. Trace the wave diagram, including the letters *T* and *C*.

7. Move the paper to the left until the right end of your traced wave touches the left end of the wave in the diagram. Make sure the fold line of the paper is lined up with the horizontal dashed line (see Figure 21.1B). Then repeat step 6.

8. Repeat step 7.

9. Refold the paper so that your traced waves show. Insert the paper into the viewer from the side with the folded edge at the top so that the waves show through the cut-out window of the viewer.

10. Move the paper strip sideways so that the letter T of one wave is centered in the cut-out window of the viewer.

11. Cut a 4 × 6-inch (10 × 15-cm) piece out of the plastic folder (discard the folder).

12. Lay the plastic piece over the window with the long side of the plastic piece along the top edge of the viewer.

13. Tape the plastic piece to the top of the viewer so that the plastic can be lifted or lowered over the window.

14. On the plastic, with the black marker, label the wave height and wavelength, as shown in Figure 21.2.

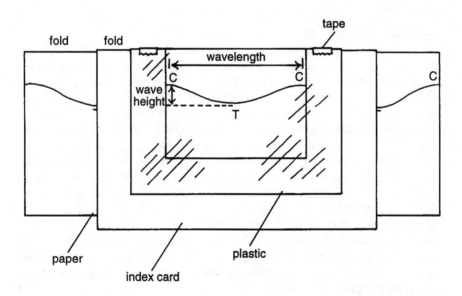

Figure 21.2

15. Hold the bottom of the viewer with one hand and pull the paper sideways through the viewer until the letter T of the next wave is centered in the window. Observe the wavelength (C to C) and the wave height (T to C) of this wave.

Results

The viewer shows three waves, each with equal wavelengths and wave heights.

Why?

A **wave** is a disturbance in a material, such as the surface of water, that repeats itself. Most waves are caused by the wind blowing across the surface of the water. Waves move across the surface of the water. The water itself does not travel with the waves but moves up and down instead.

The highest part of a wave is called the **crest** (labeled C in the model) and the lowest part is called the **trough** (T). The horizontal distance between similar points of two consecutive waves is called the **wavelength**. The vertical distance between the crest and the trough of a wave is its **wave height**.

Try New Approaches

As a wave travels through water, each water molecule moves up and down in a circular motion, ending up nearly in the same position as where it started. Repeat the experiment to prepare a model of the movement of a water molecule as a wave passes through water. Modify the plastic piece by laying it over the circle in Figure 21.3 so that the top left corner of the plastic piece matches the corner formed by the dashed lines. Trace the circle, dots, and arrows. Tape the plastic back onto the viewer. Then, holding the viewer with one hand, pull the paper sideways through the viewer with the other hand so that the top dot on the circle is centered on the crest of a wave. Slowly pull the paper in the direction of the wave, toward the right, until the bottom dot on the circle is centered on the trough of the wave. The dots on the circle represent the location of a water molecule at the crest and at the trough. The arrows indicate the direction in which the molecule moves.

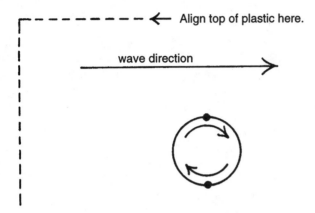

Figure 21.3

Design Your Own Experiment

1. A way to demonstrate that surface water does not move with waves is to fill a long Pyrex baking dish about three-fourths full with water. Place a small cork in the center of the water in the dish. Wait about 30 seconds to allow the water to become calm. Tap the surface of the water at one end of the dish with your finger. Observe the movement of the cork.

2. When waves come from different directions, they overlap each other. The placement of one wave atop another when they meet is called **superposition**. The waves can combine in two different ways. When crests and troughs of colliding waves match, **constructive interference** occurs. When the crests and troughs don't match, **destructive interference** occurs. Use the water-filled baking dish from the previous experiment. Simultaneously touch the surface of the water at both ends and observe the movement of the waves.

Get the Facts

While wind causes most ocean waves, underwater disturbances such as volcanoes, earthquakes, or landslides can cause freakishly long, high-speed waves called *tsunamis*. What is tsunamis' wave height in deep water? at the shore? What is their wavelength? For information about tsunamis, see Don Groves, *The Oceans* (New York: Wiley, 1989), pp. 120–122.

Percolating Water: The Movement of Water beneath the Earth's Surface

22

The amount of surface water that sinks into the ground depends on the permeability of the soil. Groundwater stops sinking when it reaches an impermeable layer.

In this project, you will demonstrate the percolation of groundwater. The effect of rainwater quantities on the level of the water table in a region is determined. You will model the upward movement of groundwater from the zone of saturation to the zone of aeration. You will also model how the pressure from an aquifer forces groundwater up through an artesian well.

Getting Started

Purpose: To model percolation of groundwater.

Materials

large spoon

2 cups (500 ml) of sand

2 cups (500 ml) of aquarium gravel or small pebbles

2-quart (2-liter) plastic or metal bowl

1-quart (1-liter) widemouthed transparent plastic jar

½ cup (125 ml) of tap water

Procedure

1. Use the spoon to mix the sand and gravel together in the bowl.

2. Spoon the sand and gravel mixture into the jar.

3. Slowly pour the water into the jar (see Figure 22.1).

4. Observe the movement of the water through the sand and gravel mixture.

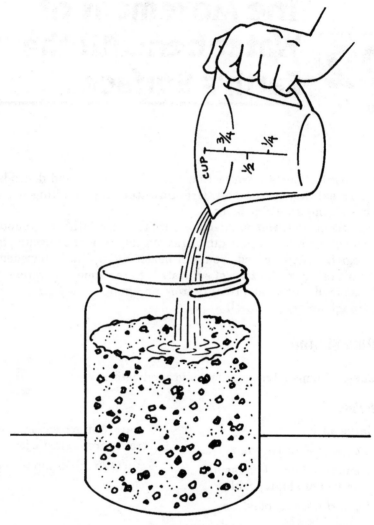

Figure 22.1

5. Allow the jar to stand in a warm area, such as a window with direct sunlight, for two or three days.

6. Observe the sand and gravel mixture, making note of its wetness.

Results

The water first wets the sand and fills the spaces between the sand and gravel in the upper part of the jar. As the water moves toward the bottom of the jar, it moves out of the spaces in the upper layer and fills the spaces in the lower layer. The upper layer becomes dry, with a wet layer below it.

Why?

Water, such as rainfall, that sinks into the ground is known as **groundwater**. This water passes through **permeable** (capable of having substances, such as fluids, move through it) materials, like the sand used in this experiment. The passing or seeping of groundwater or any liquid through a permeable material is called **percolation**.

As groundwater percolates through the ground, gravity pulls the water downward until it reaches an impermeable layer. **Impermeable** means that a fluid cannot pass through it. When the water reaches a layer that is impermeable to liquids, it spreads out as far as possible, then rises. In the experiment, the impermeable layer was the bottom of the jar. When the water reached the bottom of the jar, it spread across the glass bottom and the water level in the glass rose. At the surface of the Earth is a thin layer of moist soil from which plants receive their water. Below this moist layer, the percolation of groundwater creates two distinct underground zones. The first is called the **zone of aeration** because the pore spaces in this zone are mostly filled with air, except immediately after a rain. Rainwater fills the spaces between particles of soil, pushing the air out. The rainwater, like the water in the experiment, is pulled down by gravity and the empty pore spaces again fill with air. The **zone of saturation** lies directly below the zone of aeration. In this zone, the rocks and mineral grains are **saturated** (soaked thoroughly so that all the pore spaces are filled) with water. The boundary line between the two zones is called the **water table**. Below the water table, the pore spaces are filled with water, and above the water table, the pore spaces are filled with air. In the model, the place where the top dry layer and lower wet layer of sand and gravel meet represents the water table.

Try New Approaches

What effect does the amount of rainfall have on the height of the water table in a region? Repeat the experiment using 1 cup (225 ml) of water. **Science Fair Hint:** Make diagrams of the jar in this experiment and the one from the original experiment. Label the groundwater zones and water table in each. Indicate the amount of water added to each jar.

Design Your Own Experiment

1. Immediately above the water table, water moves from the zone of saturation up a short distance into the zone of aeration by **capillary attraction** (the attractive force between a liquid and a solid causing water to be drawn into small tubelike openings). Demonstrate that water will rise in openings between rock grains because of the attraction of the water for the rock. Do this by making eight to ten holes in the bottom of a clear plastic cup. Fill the cup with a mixture of sand and gravel. Fill a bowl with about 1 inch (2.5 cm) of water. Stand the cup of soil in the bowl. Observe the soil in the cup and the height of the water movement through the soil.

2a. An **aquifer** is a layer of permeable rock or regolith saturated with water and through which groundwater moves. A **well** (shaft sunk into the water table) in which groundwater from an aquifer rises naturally above the aquifer is called an **artesian well.** An artesian well forms when an aquifer is sandwiched between two impermeable layers. These underground layers must slope down-

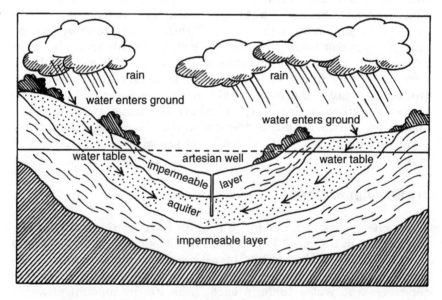

Figure 22.2

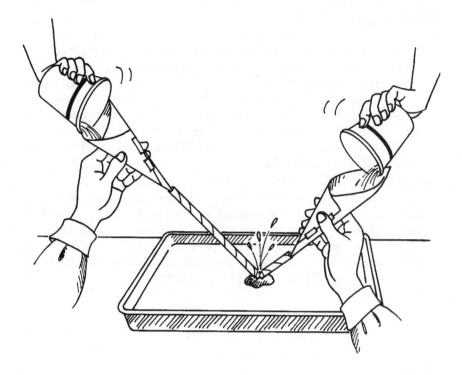

Figure 22.3

ward from their exposed surface. Water flows downward under the pull of gravity into the confined aquifer. If there is a crack leading to the surface, water escapes upward because of pressure. The pressure is due to the weight of the water in the aquifer. Make a diagram showing an aquifer between impermeable layers, such as Figure 22.2.

b. Demonstrate an artesian well by bending a flexible straw at an angle of about 110°. Make a pinhole in the straw inside the angle. Use clay to stand the bent part of the straw in a shallow baking pan. Use two 6-inch (15-cm) square pieces of waxed paper to make two cone-shaped funnels that fit into the ends of the straw. Secure the edges of the paper funnels with transparent tape. Hold the funnels in the straw ends, and ask your helper to pour water into both funnels at the same time and at the same speed. Observe the pinhole in the straw as the water enters the straw (see Figure 22.3).

Get the Facts

1. *Dissolution* is the chemical weathering process whereby minerals and rock material are dissolved by groundwater. Which types of rocks are most readily attacked by dissolution? How are caves formed? What are dripstone and flowstone? What are stalactites and stalagmites, and how are they formed? What is a sinkhole? For information about dissolution and its effects, see Brian J. Skinner and Stephen C. Porter, *The Dynamic Earth* (New York: Wiley, 1995), pp. 300–304.

2. *Adhesive force* is the attraction between unlike molecules, such as the attraction of a water molecule to a molecule on the surface of soil. *Cohesive force* is the attraction between like molecules, such as the attraction between two water molecules. How does the relationship between pore size of soil particles and adhesive and cohesive forces of water affect the permeability of the soil? For information, see *The Dynamic Earth,* pp. 286–287.

The Hydrologic Cycle: The Movement of Water from Place to Place

23

There is a continuous interchange of water between the oceans, land, plants, and clouds known as the hydrologic cycle, or water cycle. Most of this water is provided by the oceans.

In this project, you will use different water sources to model the hydrologic cycle. You will demonstrate whether dissolved pollutants in water are transported by the hydrologic cycle. The addition of water to the atmosphere by the process of transpiration will also be demonstrated.

Getting Started

Purpose: To model the hydrologic cycle.

Materials

½ cup (125 ml) of warm tap water

2-quart (2-liter) transparent Pyrex bowl

plastic food wrap

ice cube

resealable plastic sandwich bag

Procedure

1. Pour the warm water into the bowl.

2. Loosely cover the top of the bowl with plastic wrap so that about 2 inches (10 cm) of wrap extends past the edges of the bowl.

3. Put the ice cube in the bag and seal the bag.

4. Place the bag of ice in the center of the plastic wrap that covers the bowl.

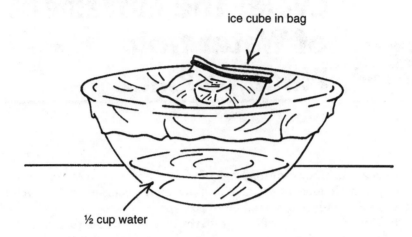

ice cube in bag

½ cup water

Figure 23.1

5. Gently push the ice down about 1 inch (2.5 cm) so that the plastic wrap sags in the center. Then, seal the plastic wrap by pressing its edge against the sides of the bowl (see Figure 23.1).

6. Observe the surface of the plastic wrap directly under the ice cube every 15 minutes for 1 hour or until the ice melts.

Results

At first, the underside of the plastic wrap becomes cloudy and water droplets form under the ice. Over time, the drops under the ice get larger and most of the plastic wrap looks clear. Some of these drops fall back into the water in the bowl.

Why?

Surface water from oceans, lakes, or any body of water is heated by the Sun, and the water vapor (water in the gas phase) formed enters the air. The phase change from liquid to gas is called **evaporation**, and the process requires energy. In the model, the energy needed for evaporation came from the warm water, but in nature, the Sun provides the energy. Water vapor in the bowl rises and comes in contact with the cool surface of the plastic wrap, where it loses energy and forms water droplets. This phase change from gas to liquid is called **condensation**. In the Earth's atmosphere, water vapor cools and condenses as it rises. The tiny drops of water form clouds, which are moved from one place to the other by winds. Eventually the water in clouds falls as **precipitation** (all forms of water that fall from the atmosphere). This movement of water from one place to another via changes in phase is called the **hydrologic cycle**, or water cycle.

The primary source of water in the hydrologic cycle is the oceans, which contain about 97% of the Earth's water supply. The remaining water comes from water evaporated from other sources such as lakes, rivers, and moist soil, and from water given off by plants in a process called **transpiration** (the loss of water by evaporation through the surface of plant leaves). About 75% of the precipitation falls back into the oceans, and much of the remaining 25% falls on the land.

Several things happen to the precipitation that reaches land. In cold areas, snow and ice can remain on the ground for short or long periods before eventually melting. Rainwater soaks into the ground or runs along the surface in rivers and streams. Some collects in lakes and other bodies of standing water, but most finds its way back to the oceans. Rainwater that is unable to soak into the ground and that moves over its surface is called **runoff**. This dissolves minerals and wears away rock, thus eroding the land as it moves. At any point, liquid water may evaporate into the atmosphere.

Try New Approaches

Model the hydrologic cycle using moist soil as a source of water. Repeat the experiment, but fill the bowl with about 1 inch (2.5 cm) of soil and add warm water to moisten the soil.

Design Your Own Experiment

1. By the process of transpiration, plants add water vapor to the air and thus contribute to the hydrologic cycle. Demonstrate transpiration by placing a clear plastic bag over a group of leaves at the end of a stem of a tree or bush. (Do not cut or break the stem off the plant.) Secure the bag to the stem by wrapping tape around the open end of the bag. Observe the contents of the bag as often as possible for two to three days. The water leaving the plant's leaves is in the gas phase. Explain the phase change in the bag. For more information about transpiration, see *Janice VanCleave's Plants* (New York: Wiley, 1997), pp. 12–15.

THE HYDROLOGIC CYCLE

Figure 23.2

2. Design a display to represent the hydrologic cycle. A sample diagram with labeled parts is shown in Figure 23.2. Colors and a legend can be used to show how *pollutants* (substances that destroy the purity of air, water, or land), such as chemical fertilizers added to the soil, can be added to waterways.

3. How does evaporation affect the concentration of dissolved pollutants in waterways? Design a way to analyze condensed water for dissolved materials. One way would be to repeat the original experiment, adding table salt to the water in the bowl. Collect the condensed water and taste it. Design a way to collect the water,

such as placing a container inside the bowl beneath the plastic wrap. Remember that when tasting materials, all supplies used must be clean.

Get the Facts

1. *Deforestation* is the clearing of trees from land. Find out how this and other human activities, such as the growth of cities and the building of dams and reservoirs, affect the hydrologic cycle. For information, see *Weather,* The Nature Company Guides (Time-Life Books, 1996), pp. 120–121.

2. About 97% of all the Earth's water is contained in the oceans as salt water. Find out about the remaining 3%, which is fresh water. How much of fresh water is locked up as ice? How much is underground? What part of fresh water is on the surface in lakes and rivers? What part is in the soil and the air? For information, see Jack Williams, *The Weather Book* (New York: Vintage Books, 1992), pp. 86–87.

Part Six

The Earth's Atmosphere

24 Atmospheric Energy: Unequal Heating by the Earth's Surface

The temperature of the Earth's atmosphere comes from the Sun's radiant energy warming the Earth's surface. The weather, climate, and seasons of a given area of the Earth depend on the temperature, which measures the energy of the atmosphere.

In this project, you will show how the directness of sunlight affects the heating of the Earth's atmosphere at the equator. You will demonstrate the effect of the Earth's shape on the unequal heating of the atmosphere. You will discover how the tilt of the Earth's axis affects the amount of sunlight that reaches different regions of the Earth's surface and thus causes different seasons. You will also see how the Earth's rotation affects atmospheric temperature.

Getting Started

Purpose: To determine why the atmosphere is warmest near the equator.

Materials

masking tape   flashlight
ruler   graph paper

Procedure

1. Tape the ruler along the side of the flashlight so that a 6-inch (15-cm) section of the ruler extends past the lamp end of the flashlight.

2. Lay the graph paper on a table.

3. Hold the flashlight perpendicular to the paper so that the free end of the ruler is on the edge of the paper and the flashlight is over the paper.

4. Darken the room and turn on the flashlight.

5. Observe the number of squares covered on the paper by the inner bright circle of light (see Figure 24.1).

163

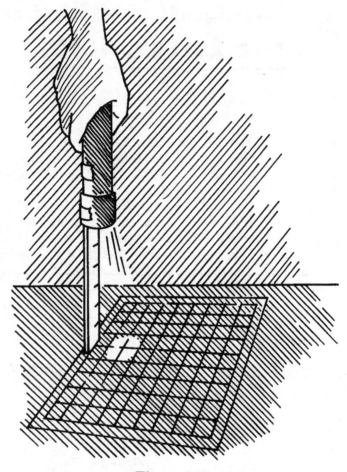

Figure 24.1

6. Tilt the ruler down so the back end of the flashlight is about 6 inches (15 cm) above the table.

7. Again observe the number of squares covered by the light.

Results

The number of squares covered by the light depends on the size of the graph paper and the size of the flashlight. But more squares are illuminated when the light is held at an angle than when it is held perpendicular to the paper. The light covers about 4 squares when the flashlight is perpendicular to the paper and about 3 times that number of squares when the flashlight is held at an angle.

Why?

Roughly the same amount of light from the flashlight struck the paper each time, but when it was more direct—perpendicular—the light was more **concentrated** (gathered together in one place) and therefore covered fewer squares. When the light was less direct—at an angle—the light was spread across more squares. The Earth's surface and its atmosphere are heated by radiant energy from the Sun. **Radiant energy** is energy that can travel through matter or space in the form of waves, which include gamma rays, X rays, ultraviolet rays, infrared rays, radio waves, and visible light. Like the perpendicular flashlight beam, the Sun's radiant energy is more concentrated near the equator and less so nearer the North and South Poles. The surface of the Earth in the equatorial region is therefore heated more by direct sunlight than are the polar regions.

The heated Earth circulates the heat back to the overlying air in the lowest part of the atmosphere called the **troposphere**. The troposphere is the region of the atmosphere where there are changes in **weather** (condition of the atmosphere in a specific place at a particular time such as pressure, temperature, humidity, winds, precipitation, and clouds). The average of weather conditions over time produces the **climate** of a given region. The equatorial region receives more direct sunlight throughout the year, so it has the warmest climate. The increase in the angle of sunlight as one approaches the Poles explains the lower temperature and hence the colder climate of the polar regions.

Try New Approaches

How does the curvature of the Earth affect the spreading of the Sun's light rays? Use the flashlight from the experiment; lay it on a table with the attached ruler extending over the table edge. Make a large cylinder out of the graph paper by overlapping the short ends. Hold the cylinder vertically at the end of the ruler. Observe the number of illuminated squares on the curved paper. Then move the cylinder slightly to the left or right so that the light grazes the edge of the cylinder. Again, observe the number of illuminated squares.

Design Your Own Experiment

1a. The temperature of the Earth's surface and thus its atmospheric temperature also change because the Earth rotates on its axis. As the Earth turns, sunlight hits a given region from different directions throughout the day. The length of shadows corresponds to the angle of sunlight. The shorter the shadow, the more direct the sunlight and the smaller the angle. A sundial tells time by casting shadows. Use a gnomon (raised part of a sundial that casts a shadow) to compare shadows during the day.

Cut a diagonal line from corner to corner across a 2-inch (5-cm) square of cardboard. Discard one of the triangles. Tape the second triangle upright to a block of wood. Set the wooden block in the center of the long side of a sheet of white poster board so that the edge of the block with the tip of the triangle is even with the edge of the poster board. As soon after sunrise as possible, place the poster board outdoors where it will receive direct sunlight all day. Using a compass, point the vertical side of the triangle north. Every hour, or as often as possible, mark a line along the edge of the triangle's shadow from the shadow's tip to the vertical end of the triangle. Mark the time of day on the poster board (see Figure 24.2). Determine the time of day when the sunlight is most direct.

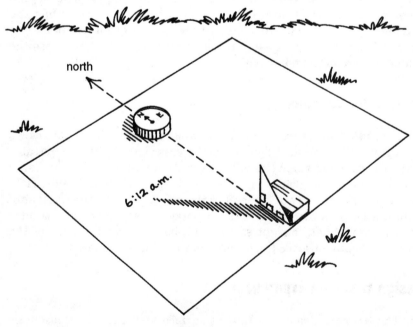

north

6:12 a.m.

Figure 24.2

b. Determine how the angle of sunlight affects atmospheric temperature by repeating the previous experiment and using a thermometer to measure air temperature each time a shadow is measured. It is best to place the thermometer out of direct sunlight to measure the air temperature.

Get the Facts

1. The number of daylight hours changes during the year. The more daylight hours during the day, the more radiant energy the Earth's surface receives. The day with the most daylight hours in the Northern Hemisphere is the first day of summer, which is on or about June 21. This day is the *summer solstice*. Find out more about the changing number of daylight hours during the year. What and when are the spring and fall equinoxes, and the winter solstice? How does the Earth's tilt cause different seasons? What is the difference between the angle of the Sun's rays in the Northern and Southern Hemispheres on these dates? What is the general difference in their atmospheric temperatures?

2. The earth's atmosphere is divided into layers. Each layer differs from the other in distance from the Earth, content, temperature, and what occurs in it. Find out more about these layers. What are their names, distances from Earth, and temperature? Where is the ozone layer, and how does it affect the type of energy that the Earth receives?

25 The Greenhouse Effect: Heat Transfer in the Atmosphere

The gases in the Earth's atmosphere are warmed by heat radiated from the Earth's surface. These warmed gases surround the Earth and act like a blanket, keeping the Earth warm.

In this project, you will demonstrate the greenhouse effect. You will discover how materials of the Earth's surface affect the greenhouse effect. You will examine the relation between the greenhouse effect and surface temperatures at night. You will determine how composition and density of the atmosphere affect its ability to trap infrared energy. You will also show how cloud cover affects the surface temperatures at night.

Getting Started

Purpose: To demonstrate the greenhouse effect.

Materials

two shoeboxes

ruler

soil

two thermometers

colorless plastic food wrap

timer

Procedure

1. Cover the bottom of each shoebox with about 2 inches (5 cm) of soil.
2. Lay a thermometer on the surface of the soil in each box.
3. Cover the opening of one box with a single layer of plastic wrap. Leave the other box uncovered.
4. Take readings from both thermometers.
5. Place both boxes side by side in a sunny place outdoors (see Figure 25.1).
6. Record readings from both thermometers every 15 minutes for 1 hour.

Figure 25.1

Results

The temperature readings show that the temperature inside the plastic-covered box was higher and increased faster.

Why?

Radiant energy from the Sun passes through the Earth's atmosphere and reaches the Earth's surface. However, about 30% of the Sun's total radiant energy reaching the Earth is reflected back into space by the atmosphere, the clouds, and the Earth's surface. About 20% is absorbed by the atmosphere, and the remaining 50% is absorbed by the Earth's surface. Radiant energy absorbed by the Earth is changed into heat or **infrared rays** (invisible form of radiant energy that has a heating effect). Some of this heat from the Earth warms the atmosphere above it. This heat is transferred to the atmosphere by **conduction** (transfer of heat by direct contact between materials), **convection** (transfer of heat by the movement of heated **fluids**—gases and liquids), and **radiation** (transfer of heat by emission of heat waves). Carbon dioxide and water vapor are gases in the atmosphere that help keep heat from being lost to space. They absorb heat from the Earth and **reradiate** (emit previously absorbed radiation) it toward the Earth. Like the plastic covering that prevents the escape of some of the infrared rays radiated from the soil, the Earth's atmosphere keeps the Earth warm. The term **greenhouse effect** comes from the fact that the atmosphere is similar to a greenhouse in that it helps warm the Earth's surface by trapping infrared energy.

Try New Approaches

1. What effect do surface materials have on the greenhouse effect? Repeat the original experiment, preparing boxes with different surfaces by covering the soil with different materials, such as sand, rocks, and grass. A surface of water could be prepared by lining the box with plastic and filling it with about 2 inches (5 cm) of water instead of soil. **Science Fair Hint:** Display photographs of the various boxes with the results of the experiment. Include a display, such as the one shown in Figure 25.2, indicat-

REFLECTED SOLAR ENERGY

Figure 25.2

ing the percentage of radiant energy reflected back into space. For information about reflected radiant energy, see Jack Williams, *The Weather Book* (New York: Vintage Books, 1992), p. 19.

2. What is the relation between the greenhouse effect and surface temperatures at night, in the absence of the Sun's radiant energy? Repeat the original experiment, taking temperature readings while the boxes are in direct sunlight outdoors. Then place the boxes in a dark area indoors. Again, take readings from both thermometers every 15 minutes for 1 hour.

3a. Could the composition of the atmosphere affect its ability to trap infrared energy? Compare different materials for their ability to trap infrared energy. Repeat the original experiment using plastic wrap and other materials, such as waxed paper, clear Plexiglas, and glass. **Science Fair Hint:** Display samples of the box covers with the results of the experiment.

b. Density is the mass of a substance per unit volume. The greater the density of a substance, the closer together its particles. How does the density of the atmosphere affect its ability to trap infrared energy? Repeat the previous experiment twice, first using two layers of material, then using three layers. **Science Fair Hint:** Compare the results of the experiment to surface environments on celestial bodies with little or no atmosphere, such as the Moon and Mars, and those with a dense atmosphere, such as Venus. Use an astronomy text to find out about the atmosphere of the different celestial bodies. Make charts showing the composition and density of their atmosphere and surface environment.

Design Your Own Experiment

1. Design a way to determine how the Earth's atmosphere affects the surface air temperature at night. One way is to record air temperature at sunset and again at sunrise for one or more weeks in a chart similar to Table 25.1. Calculate the difference between the two temperatures each day, and determine an average by adding the differences and dividing by the total number of days. *Note:* Your temperature measurements should be taken during a time of a constant weather pattern.

2. Repeat the previous experiment to determine how cloud cover affects surface temperature during the night. Do this by recording

Table 25.1 Day and Night Temperatures, °F (°C)			
Day	Sunset	Sunrise	Difference
1	80° (26.7°)	62° (16.7°)	18° (10°)
2	82° (27.8°)	61° (16.1°)	21° (11.7°)
7	80° (26.7°)	63° (17.2°)	17° (9.5°)

air temperature during cloudy and noncloudy periods. On four or more days on which the weather forecast calls for the same amount of nighttime cloud cover, record the temperature at sunset and again at sunrise. Repeat by recording the day and night temperatures on four or more days with little or no nighttime cloud cover. Use the results to determine how the presence or absence of clouds in the troposphere leads to more heat escaping to space, thus causing a greater decrease in nighttime temperature.

Get the Facts

Carbon dioxide, one of the greenhouse gases, is responsible for much of the warming of the Earth. Some scientists predict a rise in the average temperature of the Earth if the amount of carbon dioxide in the atmosphere continues to increase. Find out more about the production of carbon dioxide. How do fossil fuel emissions and deforestation affect the level of carbon dioxide in the atmosphere? What is insolation and how does it affect global warming? For information about the greenhouse effect and greenhouse gases, see *Janice VanCleave's Ecology for Every Kid* (New York: Wiley, 1996), pp. 139–146.

Convection: Air in Motion

The movement of air molecules from one place to another is due to differences in energy of the air in each area. More energetic air molecules are warmer, faster and less dense than less energetic air molecules. In response to changes in temperature, air molecules move faster and spread apart, or move slower and get closer together.

In this project, you will demonstrate how convection currents are produced as a result of differences in temperature. You will determine why air pollution increases during an air condition called inversion. You will demonstrate the effect that temperature has on the density of air and use the results to explain why cold air is more dense than warm air. You will also model a convection cell to learn how updrafts and downdrafts are produced.

Getting Started

Purpose: To demonstrate how convection currents are produced.

Materials

2-inch (5-cm) piece of mosquito coil and a coil stand (found where camping supplies are sold)

matches

two 1-quart (1-liter) glass jars with equal-size mouths

3 × 5-inch (7.5 × 12.5-cm) index card

desk lamp

9 × 12-inch (22.5 × 30-cm) sheet of black construction paper

transparent tape

Note: This experiment requires access to a freezer.

Procedure

CAUTION: *Get adult approval to handle the burning mosquito coil and candle in this chapter.*

1. Follow the package instructions to place the coil in the mosquito coil stand and to ignite the end of the coil. This should be done on an outdoor table.

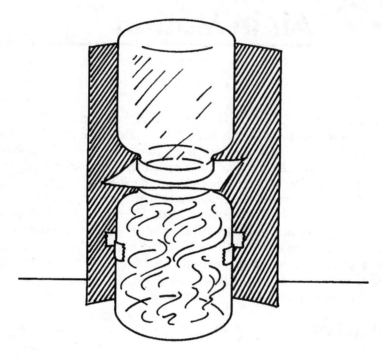

Figure 26.1

2. Invert one of the jars and stand it over the burning coil for 2 to 3 minutes or until the jar is filled with smoke.

3. Lift the jar and cover its mouth with the index card.

4. Take the jar indoors and place it on a table near a desk lamp.

5. Place the second, empty jar in the freezer for 2 minutes.

6. Remove the jar from the freezer. Invert the cold jar and stand it mouth to mouth on the smoke-filled jar, with the index card between them.

7. Stand the black paper behind the jars and secure it to the bottom jar with tape (see Figure 26.1).

8. Slightly lift the top jar, remove the index card, and place the jar mouths together. Do this with as little movement to the bottom jar as possible.

9. Position the lamp so that the smoke is as visible as possible.

10. Observe the contents of the two jars.

Results

The smoke in the bottom jar rises and fills the top jar.

Why?

The air in the bottom jar is warmer than the air in the top jar. Warm-air molecules have more energy and move around faster than do less energetic cold-air molecules. The speedy warm-air molecules tend to move away from each other. So warm air, with its molecules spaced farther apart, is less **dense** (compact) and lighter than cold air with its molecules closer together. While in the freezer, the open jar filled with cold, dense air. When the card was removed, the heavy cold air sank and the light warm air rose. The smoke was lifted with the rising warm air. This up-and-down movement of air due to differences in temperature is called **convection currents**.

Try New Approaches

1a. An **inversion** is a layer of warm air lying above a layer of cold air in the atmosphere. Repeat the experiment standing the cold jar on the table and inverting the warm smoke-filled jar.

b. Repeat the experiment sealing the jar of smoke with a lid and placing it in the refrigerator. Remove the jar from the refrigerator, then remove the lid and cover the jar with the index card. Stand the jars together as before, but with the cold, smoky jar on the bottom and the other jar inverted on top. Use the results to determine why air pollution near the ground increases during an inversion and can cause serious health problems.

Design Your Own Experiment

1. Demonstrate the effect that temperature has on the density of air by inflating a balloon and tying the end. Use a measuring tape to measure the circumference of the largest part of the balloon. While the tape is wrapped around the balloon, ask a helper to use a marker to draw a line on the balloon along one edge of the tape. Place the balloon in the freezer for 10 minutes. Remove the balloon, and again use the measuring tape to measure the circumference of the balloon along the line drawn around the balloon. Note any change in the size of the balloon. Place the balloon in a bowl of hot water, turning the balloon in the water often for 2 to 3 min-

Figure 26.2

utes. Dry the balloon, and again measure and note any size changes. Use the results to explain why cold air is more dense than warm air.

2. **Wind** is the movement of air in a general horizontal direction. Most winds are caused by convection. A **convection cell** is a pattern of air circulation caused by unequal heating of the Earth's surface. At one end of the cell is a zone of rising air, called **updrafts**, and at the other end is a zone of sinking air, called **downdrafts**. Create a convection cell by cutting a piece of aluminum foil large enough to cover the top of a large glass container, such as a 10-gallon (40-liter) aquarium. Use heavy-duty aluminum foil to make two tubes about the size of a toilet tissue tube. Cut two holes at opposite ends of the aluminum foil cover large enough to hold the tubes. Place the cover over the glass container. One at a time, place the tubes in the holes and use masking tape to secure and seal any cracks around the tubes. Lifting one end of the foil cover, place a candle below one of the tubes and a 2-inch (5-cm) piece of mosquito coil in a stand between the two tubes. Ignite the candle and the mosquito coil. Secure the foil cover on the aquarium by squeezing the edges tightly to its sides (see Figure 26.2). Observe the movement of the smoke in the

aquarium. *Note:* The coil produces only a small amount of heat in comparison to that given off by the candle.

From the results, determine the following:

- Which air temperature, warm or cold, produces updrafts? Which temperature produces downdrafts?

- At ground level, does the air move from the updraft to the downdraft, or vice versa?

Extinguish the candle by lifting the end of foil cover opposite the candle and blowing into the container.

CAUTION: *The air and foil above the burning candle can be hot enough to burn your skin.*

Get the Facts

Updrafts cool at a rate of about 5.4°F (−14.7°C) per 1,000 feet (300 m), and downdrafts warm at the same rate. Find out more about why air changes temperature at different altitudes. How does pressure affect the temperature of updrafts and downdrafts? How are the dry Santa Ana winds in California and the Chinook winds in the Rockies produced? For information about updrafts and downdrafts, see Jack Williams, *The Weather Book* (New York: Vintage Books, 1992), pp. 69–70.

27 | Fronts: Moving Air Masses

Masses of air that stay in place for a length of time take on the characteristics of temperature and humidity of the region of the Earth beneath them. The temperature and humidity differences between adjoining regions result in movement of air masses and changes in local weather.

In this project, you will learn about air masses and demonstrate how differences in their density cause warm and cold fronts. You will learn how source regions give rise to the names of air masses and how these names can be combined to describe the humidity and temperature of the source region. You will discover how symbols on weather maps indicate movement of fronts and how clouds can be used to identify fronts. You will study dew point and how this temperature is affected by fronts, and its effect on cloud formation.

Getting Started

Purpose: To model a warm front.

Materials

1-cup (250-ml) measuring cup

tap water

blue food coloring

spoon

one 20-ounce (600-ml) clear plastic bottle

1 cup (250 ml) of liquid cooking oil

Procedure

1. Fill the measuring cup with water.
2. Add three drops of food coloring to the water and stir.
3. Pour the water into the bottle.
4. Fill the measuring cup with oil.
5. Tilt the bottle and slowly pour the oil into the bottle (see Figure 27.1).
6. Observe the movement of the oil into the bottle.

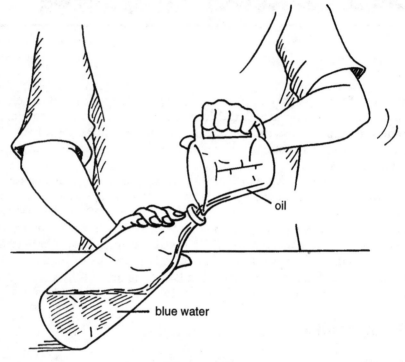

Figure 27.1

Results

The oil moves across the top of the blue water.

Why?

An **air mass** is a large body of air with about the same temperature and humidity throughout. Air masses form when air stays over a region long enough to take on the temperature and humidity characteristics of that region. It takes a week or more for an air mass to form.

The density of air masses varies with the temperature and humidity of the air. Warm air masses are less dense than cold air masses, and humid air masses are less dense than dry air masses. When air masses with different densities meet, the two masses do not mix. As with oil and water, a distinct boundary forms between the air masses. In the experiment, the oil represented a warm air mass and the colored water a cold air mass. As with the oil and water, warm, less dense air moves over cold, denser air.

Vilhelm Bjerknes (1862–1951), a Norwegian physicist and meteorologist, coined the term **front** to describe the boundary between warm and cold air masses. The leading edge of a warm air mass advancing into a region occupied by a cold air mass is called a **warm front**. A **cold front** occurs when a cold air mass advances into a region occupied by a warm air mass. If the boundary between the cold and warm air masses doesn't move, it is called a **stationary front**. The boundary where a cold air mass meets a cool air mass under a warm air mass is called an **occluded front**. At a front, the weather is usually unsettled and stormy, and precipitation is common.

Try New Approaches

1. Model a cold front produced by the movement of a cold air mass into a region occupied by a warm air mass. Do this by repeating the experiment, but place the oil in the bottle first, then slowly pour in the colored water.

2. Does the volume of the air masses affect the results? Repeat the original experiment twice, first using 1½ cups (375 ml) of water and ½ cup (125 ml) of oil, then using ½ cup (125 ml) of water and 1½ cups (375 ml) of oil.

Design Your Own Experiment

1. The region where air masses form is called a **source region**. The four source regions are ocean, land, tropics, and Poles. An air mass that forms over an ocean is called a **maritime air mass**. This type of air mass is generally humid. An air mass that forms over land is called a **continental air mass** and tends to be dry. An air mass that forms near the Poles is called a **polar air mass** and tends to be cold. An air mass that forms over the **tropics**, or **horse latitudes** (region between latitudes 23½° N and 23½° S) is called a **tropical air mass** and tends to be warm. These names of air masses can be combined to describe two characteristics—the humidity and the temperature of the source region. For example, a continental polar air mass forms over land near the Poles and tends to be dry and cold. Prepare a display representing the different source regions of air masses and their characteristics.

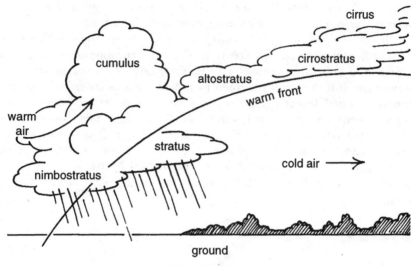

Figure 27.2

2. **Clouds** are visible atmospheric masses, consisting of a high **concentration** (amount of substance dissolved or mixed in a specified quantity of a solution or mixture) of minute water droplets or ice crystals in air. Clouds can be used to identify the type of an approaching front. Use an earth science text to identify the types of clouds present at each front. Prepare drawings similar to Figure 27.2, and use them to compare the clouds associated with each type of front, and the shape and movement of air masses of each type of front. For descriptions of cloud types, see *National Audubon Society Field Guide to North American Weather* (New York: Knopf, 1995), pp. 79–92.

3a. At the frontal area, air rises or is lifted. Air cools as it rises, eventually reaching **dew point**, which is the temperature at which water vapor condenses. At the dew point, the invisible water vapor in air condenses on cool surfaces in a collection of tiny water drops that form clouds. Show how cloud water droplets form by condensation by filling a glass with ice, then adding enough water to cover the ice. Observe the outside of the glass for the **condensate** (liquid formed by condensation).

b. Measure the dew point by repeating the previous experiment, placing a thermometer in the glass. Determine the temperature at which the water vapor in the air condenses on the glass.

Get the Facts

1. The *jet stream* is a narrow band of high-speed wind in the upper atmosphere. Its general direction is from west to east. How does the position of the jet stream affect the movement of air masses? For information about jet streams, see *National Audubon Society Field Guide to North American Weather* (New York: Knopf, 1995), p. 47.

2. *Meterologists* are scientists who study the atmosphere and how it behaves. They gather information and prepare detailed weather maps. Symbols are used to show each bit of information. Weather maps appear daily in the newspaper. What symbols on the maps are used to represent the different fronts? How is the direction of a front represented? For information about weather map symbols for fronts, see Jack Williams, *The Weather Book* (New York: Vintage Books, 1992), p. 45.

Barometric Changes: The Cause and Measurement of Air Pressure

28

Atmospheric pressure is the measure of the pressure that the atmosphere exerts on surfaces. Since the atmosphere is composed of air, the term *air pressure* is sometimes used. Weather forecasters measure atmospheric pressure with barometers and use the term *barometric pressure*.

In this project, you will make different barometers and use them to measure and compare atmospheric pressure in different places and at different times. You will demonstrate how the impact of air molecules exerts atmospheric pressure. You will show how air with greater density exerts greater atmospheric pressure. You will also learn about the relation between barometric pressure at sea level and at higher altitudes as well as natural barometers.

Getting Started

Purpose: To show how a barometer works.

Materials

serrated knife (use with
  adult approval)

scissors

masking tape

two 20-ounce (600-ml)
  plastic bottles

one-hole paper punch

flexible straw

tap water

Procedure

1. Cut off the top 3 inches (7.5 cm) of one of the bottles. Do this by sawing a small slit in the bottle with the knife, then use the scissors to cut around the bottle. Keep the bottom section.

2. Cover the cut edges of the bottle with tape.

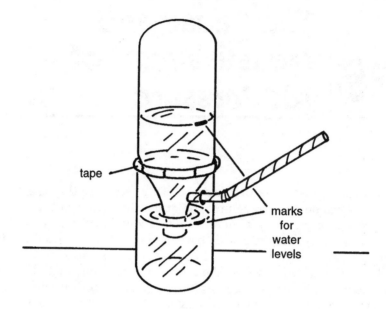

Figure 28.1

3. Use the paper punch to make a hole about 1 inch (2.5 cm) from the cut edge of the bottle.

4. Insert about ½ inch (1.25 cm) of the straw through the hole. The straw should fit snugly in the hole.

5. Stand the cut and uncut bottles side by side. Fill the bottles half full with equal amounts of water.

6. With your fingers over the mouth of the uncut bottle, turn it upside down, then lower it into the cut bottle. The mouth of the bottle should be below the water level in the cut bottle, and the two bottles should fit snugly together. The combined bottles form a barometer.

7. Near the straw, use the marking pen to mark the water lines on both bottles (see Figure 28.1).

8. Blow into the straw and observe the change in the water level in each bottle.

9. Suck air out of the straw, and again observe the change in the water level in each bottle.

Results

Blowing into the straw causes the water to rise above the water line in the top bottle and sink below the line in the bottom bottle. The reverse is true when air is sucked out of the straw: the water sinks below the water line in the top bottle and rises above it in the bottom bottle.

Why?

Atmospheric pressure, also called air pressure, is the force that air exerts on a particular area. It is a measure of the pressure resulting from the **force** (push or pull exerted on matter) that the total mass of air in an imaginary column exerts on a horizontal area. The greater the mass—that is, the greater the number of molecules—the greater the air pressure.

Atmospheric pressure is directly related to the density of air, which measures the number of air molecules in a given space. This was demonstrated by the barometer you made in this experiment. A **barometer** is an instrument used to measure atmospheric pressure. Before you blew air into or sucked air out of the straw, the atmospheric pressure pushing down on the water's surface in the lower bottle was equal to the air pressure pushing down on the water in the upper bottle. Blowing into the straw increased the amount of air in the lower bottle; thus the pressure on the surface of the water in this bottle increased. This increase in pressure forced water from the lower bottle into the upper bottle. The water level in the lower bottle sank, and the level in the upper bottle rose. The reverse happened when air was removed from the lower bottle. The pressure pushing down on the water in the lower bottle decreased, and the pressure in the upper bottle pushed water down into the lower bottle. The water level in the upper bottle sank, and the level in the lower bottle rose.

Try New Approaches

1a. Does atmospheric pressure outside the bottle barometer change enough to affect the water levels in the bottles? Make a scale by sticking a 3-inch (7.5-cm) strip of masking tape along the side of and centered over the mark of the top bottle. Use a fine-point pen and a ruler to mark a line in the center of the tape over the mark on the bottle. Continue to mark lines 1/16 inch (2 mm) apart above and below the center line. Number the center line 0. Number the tenth mark below the line −1 and the next tenth mark −2. Continue to the end of the tape. Repeat, using positive numbers above the center line. Set the barometer inside your home where it will not be disturbed. Leave the straw open. At the same time each day for seven or more days, record the water level on the scale in the top bottle.

b. Does the atmospheric pressure outside your house differ from the pressure inside? Repeat the original experiment, making a second bottle barometer. Then, repeat the previous experiment, placing one barometer inside and the other outside. **Science Fair Hint:** Record the atmospheric pressure from a local television or radio weather program. Prepare a diagram showing the bottle barometer's readings and the recorded atmospheric pressure for each day.

2. Does atmospheric pressure change during the day? Use the bottle barometer to record the water level and time every hour for 6 or more hours during one day. Use the information to prepare a bar graph showing the pattern of change.

Design Your Own Experiment

1. Prepare another type of barometer by cutting the top from a 12-inch (30-cm) round balloon. Stretch the bottom section of the balloon across the top of a wide-mouthed 1-quart (1-liter) jar, and secure it with a rubber band. Cut one end of a drinking straw to a point. Glue the uncut end of the straw to the center of the stretched balloon. Secure a metric ruler to another 1-quart (1-liter) jar with a rubber band. The ruler must stand upright, with the zero end of the metric scale at the bottom. (The marks on the metric scale are close, allowing small pressure changes to be measured.) Position the two jars so that the pointed end of the straw points to the metric markings on the ruler. Do not allow the straw to touch the ruler (see Figure 28.2). Repeat the previous experiments replacing the bottle barometer with this jar barometer.

2a. Air is made up of gas molecules, mostly nitrogen and oxygen. These molecules move and hit against each other and anything that gets in their path. The impacts of these bouncing molecules cause pressure. Demonstrate how the impact of an air molecule causes atmospheric pressure by dropping a marble on a scale. Use a scale with a 1-pound (454-g) capacity. Place the scale in the

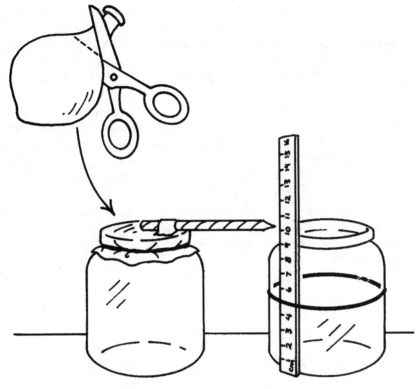

Figure 28.2

center of a box that is about 1 foot (30 cm) long and wide and about 6 inches (15 cm) taller than the scale. Hold a marble about 6 inches (15 cm) above the scale and drop it. (The box just needs to be large enough to contain the marble when it falls off the scale.) Observe the movement of the scale's dial.

b. Air molecules are in constant motion. Like air molecules hitting against a surface, enough marbles hitting the scale in succession would keep the scale indicator from moving back to zero. Design a method to drop a series of marbles, such as rolling them down a folded piece of cardboard toward the scale.

Get the Facts

1. Evangelista Torricelli (1608–1647), an Italian mathematician and physicist, discovered the principle of a barometer in 1643. An encyclopedia can be used to find out about the experiment that Torricelli did to discover how the pressures of air could be measured. A water barometer was invented by Otto von Guericke (1602–1686), the mayor of Magdeburg, Germany, in 1646. How did Guericke's barometer compare to the barometer designed by Torricelli?

2. Aneroid barometers are inexpensive and commonly found in homes and offices. *Aneroid* is from a Greek word meaning "without liquid." Find out how this barometer measures air pressure. For information about aneroid barometers, see Frank H. Forrester, *1001 Questions Answered about the Weather* (New York: Dover Publications, 1981), p. 17.

3. Barometric pressure increases at altitudes above sea level. What causes this difference in pressure due to altitude? For information, see *The Nature Company Guides: Weather* (Time Life Books, 1996), p. 26.

Hygrometers: Ways to Measure the Atmosphere's Water Content

29

An instrument that measures the humidity of air is called a hygrometer. The efficiency of the instrument depends on its hygroscopic (water-attracting) nature.

In this project, you will make hygrometers and use them to measure and compare the hygroscopic quality of different papers and to indicate differences in humidity. Hygrometer scales will be designed to give more accurate humidity measurements. You will study how things in nature, such as pine cones, indicate changes in humidity. You will also construct a psychrometer and use it to measure relative humidity.

Getting Started

Purpose: To make a hygrometer.

Materials

scissors

ruler

lightweight aluminum foil

newspaper

transparent tape

two short pencils about 6 inches (15 cm) long

masking tape

marking pen

two 1-quart (1-liter) jars with lids

tap water

two thread spools

hair dryer

timer

Procedure

1. Cut a piece of aluminum foil about 4 × 12 inches (10 × 30 cm).
2. Cut a strip of newspaper 1 × 10 inches (2.5 × 25 cm).
3. Lay the newspaper strip in the center of the aluminum piece.

4. Tape the edges of the paper to the foil with a single layer of tape.

5. Trim the foil around the newspaper edges, leaving about ¼ inch (0.63 cm) of foil on all sides.

6. Tape one end of the strip to the center of one pencil.

7. Repeat steps 1 through 6 to prepare a second strip.

8. Use the masking tape and pen to label one jar "humid" and the other "dry."

9. Pour about 1 inch (2.5 cm) of hot tap water into the "humid" jar, stand one thread spool in the jar, then secure the lid.

10. Use the hair dryer to heat the inside of the "dry" jar for about 30 seconds, stand the second thread spool in the jar, then secure the lid.

11. Use the hair dryer to thoroughly dry the newspaper on the strips.

12. Wind the strips snugly around the pencils so that the aluminum foil is on the outside.

13. Open each jar and stand the pencils in the holes in the thread spools, then again secure the lids on the jars (see Figure 29.1).

14. After 1 hour, remove the pencil-spool sets from each jar and observe the strip around each.

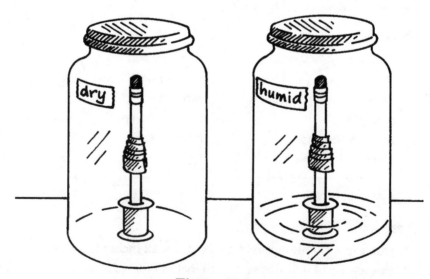

Figure 29.1

Results

The coil of paper unwinds slightly in the humid jar and the coil makes little or no change in the dry jar.

Why?

The newspaper is **hygroscopic**, which means it absorbs water from the air. The water molecules may be held in pores and imperfections in the paper. As the pores in the paper fill with water, the paper expands and pushes against the aluminum foil, which is not hygroscopic. The force of the expanding paper causes the coil to unwind.

Humidity is the amount of water vapor or moisture in the air. The air in the jar above the warm water has a high humidity. This is due to the increased rate of water evaporation from the warm water's surface. All or most of the water in the air in the heated jar evaporated and left the jar. Thus, the air in this jar has a low humidity. The paper coils act as **hygrometers** (instruments used to measure the amount of water or humidity in the air). The more humid the air, the more water the coil can absorb and the more the coil expands.

Try New Approaches

1. Is some paper more hygroscopic than others? Repeat the experiment comparing the results of papers such as construction paper and typing paper with newspaper. Use the most hygroscopic paper for the following experiment.

2. Can the coil be used to indicate changes in air humidity? Place one of the coils inside a dry open jar and the other in a dry closed jar. Stand the jars outdoors on different days with low, medium, and high humidity. (The jars prevent any wind from unwinding the coils.) Compare the tightness of the coils to determine the size of the coils when the air has low, medium, and high humidity. How accurate is this method of measuring humidity?

Design Your Own Experiment

1. Design a hygrometer with a scale, such as one using a hygroscopic strand of silk or hair. (Silk threads can be found where embroidery floss is sold.) One possible design is to cut a pointer from stiff paper and punch two opposite holes in the pointer. Hang the pointer by the hole near its straight end on a nail secured to a

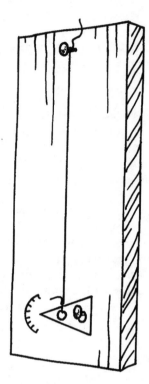

Figure 29.2

board. Cut a hygroscopic strand about 10 inches (25 cm) long, and tie one end to the other hole in the pointer. Hold the free end of the strand against the board so that the straight end of the pointer is parallel to the edge of the board. Secure a second nail to the board near the end of the strand, and tie the strand to the nail. Use a fine-tipped pen and a metric ruler to mark a few lines at 1-cm intervals at the tip of the pointer, as shown in Figure 29.2. Observe the effect of changes in humidity on the hygroscopic strand.

2. **Relative humidity** is the ratio between the amount of water vapor present in the air and the amount of water vapor the air can hold at that temperature, expressed as a percentage. A **psychrometer** is a type of hygrometer used to measure relative humidity. A psychrometer has two thermometers, a wet-bulb thermometer and a dry-bulb thermometer. Make a psychrometer

Table 29.1   Relative Humidity in Air

Difference between Dry-Bulb and Wet-Bulb Temperatures (°C)

Dry-Bulb Temperature (°C)	1	2	3	4	5	6	7	8	9	10	11	12	13	14	15	16
0	81	64	46	29	13											
2	84	68	52	37	22	7										
4	85	71	57	43	29	16										
6	86	73	60	48	35	24	11									
8	87	75	63	51	40	29	19	8								
10	88	77	66	55	44	34	24	15	6							
12	89	78	68	58	48	39	29	21	12							
14	90	79	70	60	51	42	34	26	18	10						
16	90	81	71	63	54	46	38	30	23	15	8					
18	91	82	73	65	57	49	41	34	27	20	14	7				
20	91	83	74	66	59	51	44	37	31	24	18	12	6			
22	92	83	76	68	61	54	47	40	34	28	22	17	11	6		
24	92	84	77	69	62	56	49	43	37	31	26	20	15	10	5	
26	92	85	78	71	64	58	51	46	40	34	29	24	19	14	10	5

by wrapping the bulb of one thermometer with a thin layer of wet cotton and leaving the second thermometer uncovered. Lay the two thermometers on the edge of a table with their bulbs extending over the table edge. With an index card, fan the air near the two thermometers, but do not touch the thermometers with the card. When the wet-bulb thermometer reaches its lowest point, record the temperature on both thermometers. Use the following example and the relative humidity table, Table 29.1, to determine relative humidity from your psychrometer readings. *Note:* If your thermometer measures in degrees Fahrenheit, use Appendix 2 to **convert** (change) degrees Fahrenheit to degrees Celsius.

Example:
What is the relative humidity if the dry-bulb reading is 16°C and the wet-bulb reading is 13°C?

- Subtract the wet-bulb temperature from the dry-bulb temperature:

$$16°C - 13°C = 3°C$$

- Find 16, the dry-bulb temperature, in the column on the left side of Table 29.1, and 3, the difference between the dry-bulb and wet-bulb temperatures, in the horizontal row at the top of the table. Where the column and row meet is the number for the relative humidity. For this example, the number is 71; thus the relative humidity is 71%.

For more information about relative humidity and psychrometers, see *National Audubon Society Field Guide to North American Weather* (New York: Chanticleer Press, 1995), pp. 607–608.

Get the Facts

1. *Dew point* is the temperature at which air cannot hold any more water and condensation occurs. Find out more about dew point. What does the saturation point of air mean? How does temperature affect air's saturation point? See *Weather,* The Nature Company Guides (New York: Time Life Books, 1996), pp. 40–41.

2. *Hygrometry* is the science of determining how much water air can hold at a given temperature and pressure. Scientific instruments, such as hygrometers, are used to make these measurements. But nature also provides its own hygrometers. If the humidity is very high, the cone scales of a pinecone close, as do the petals of the flower of the scarlet pimpernel. See Gary Lockhart, *The Weather Companion* (New York: Wiley, 1988) pp. 27–30. Find out more about how natural hygrometers affect the opening and closing of pinecones. For information, see *The Weather Companion,* pp. 27–30.

Precipitation: Phases of Atmospheric Water

30

Precipitation is the falling of water in either a solid or a liquid phase. The phase of precipitation depends on the temperature of the atmosphere in which the precipitation forms or through which it is falling.

In this project, you will measure and compare the size of drizzle drops and raindrops. You will determine the effect of condensation nuclei on the formation of water drops. You will demonstrate how cloud drops grow by coalescence. You will learn about the formation of different frozen precipitation. You will also learn about the hexagonal organization of freezing water in the formation of snowflakes.

Getting Started

Purpose: To determine how to measure raindrop sizes.

Materials

1 cup (250 ml) of flour	large bowl
wire strainer	sheet of construction paper, any dark color
cake pan	
spray bottle	pencil
tap water	metric ruler
large serving spoon	magnifying lens

Procedure

1. Sift the flour through the strainer into the cake pan. Discard any flour particles that do not fall through the strainer.

2. Fill the spray bottle with water.

3. Set the pan on a table, and spray a mist of water from the spray bottle so that it falls on the surface of the flour (see Figure 30.1).

4. Use the spoon to dip one or two spoonfuls of flour from the pan into the strainer. Dip the drops of water along with the flour.

Figure 30.1

5. Hold the strainer over the bowl and gently shake it back and forth so that the flour falls through the holes in the strainer and into the bowl. Shake until all loose flour falls into the bowl and balls of flour remain in the strainer.

6. Pour the flour balls from the strainer onto the paper.

7. Repeat steps 4 through 6 until all the flour in the pan has been sifted and flour balls collected.

8. Measure the size of several of the flour balls one ball at a time by using the tip of the pencil to move each ball next to the ruler.

9. Observe the ball and ruler through the magnifying lens. Move the ruler so that the left side of the ball is in line with a measuring mark.

Results

A variety of different sizes of flour balls are formed.

Why?

The water from the spray mist falls like raindrops on the surface of the flour. When the drops hit the flour's surface, fine particles of flour coat the outside of the drop. Thus, separate flour balls are formed that are filled with water. The flour coating on each water drop slightly increases the size of the drop of water.

Try New Approaches

CAUTION: *Do not do the following experiments when there is lightning.*

1a. Do raindrops vary in size? Repeat the experiment, placing the pan of flour in the rain for a short time.

b. Rain and drizzle are forms of precipitation. In comparison to rain, **drizzle** has very fine droplets of liquid water that fall very close together and very slowly. Do drops of drizzle vary in size? Repeat the previous experiment during a drizzle. **Science Fair Hint:** Make diagrams to compare the size of the drops of drizzle to raindrops.

Design Your Own Experiment

1. **Condensation nuclei** are small particles that attract water and encourage condensation. Most precipitation begins as water vapor condensing around condensation nuclei. Demonstrate the effect of condensation nuclei on the formation of water drops by covering the bottom of a saucer with water. Cut a circle from black construction paper large enough to cover the inside of a jar lid that is about 2 inches (5 cm) in diameter. Place the circle in the lid and cover the paper with a thin layer of petroleum jelly. This will aid in preventing the paper from absorbing water. Sprinkle eight to ten salt grains on the oiled paper. Use a pencil to separate the grains. Set the lid in the saucer of water and cover with a 10-ounce (300-ml) plastic cup (see Figure 30.2). Observe the salt grains through a magnifying lens every 30 minutes for 3 hours. Observe the grains again after 24 hours. Find out more about condensation nuclei. Make a model representing the general size of condensation nuclei. Information about condensation nuclei can be found in Jack Williams, *The Weather Book* (New York: Vintage Books, 1992), pp. 66–67.

2. Condensation produces **cloud drops**, which are drops of water with diameters between 0.00004 and 0.002 inches (0.0001 and 0.0005 cm) in clouds. In order to produce raindrops heavy enough

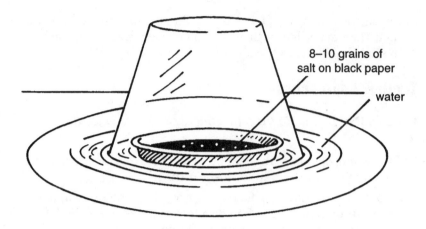

8–10 grains of
salt on black paper

water

Figure 30.2

to fall, the cloud drops must grow. Growth of cloud drops in clouds with temperatures above freezing occurs by **coalescence**, which is the merging of water drops that collide. Demonstrate this by filling an eyedropper with water. Hold a plastic lid in your hand so that it is parallel to the ground. Squeeze out of the eyedropper as many separate drops of water as will fit on the top of the lid. Quickly turn the lid upside down and right side up. Many of the larger water drops will fall off the lid, but use the point of a pencil to move the remaining smaller drops of water together into larger drops. Turn the lid upside again, and continue combining drops until they all fall.

Get the Facts

1. Precipitation formed in clouds with temperatures above freezing is called *warm precipitation*. If ice is involved at some stage in the production, the precipitation is called *cold precipitation*. For more information about warm and cold precipitation, see "precipitation" in Grolier Multimedia, Encarta, or other CD-ROM encyclopedias.

2. *Weather modification* is the changing of the atmospheric environment in some artificial way. Artificial rainmaking is accomplished by *cloud seeding,* which is the artificial addition of con-

densation nuclei to clouds. Find out more about cloud seeding. What are clouds seeded with? See Frank H. Forrester, *1001 Questions Answered about the Weather* (New York: Dover Publications, 1981), pp. 358–359.

3. *Drizzle* is drops of liquid water with a diameter less than 0.02 inches (0.005 cm). Find out more about liquid precipitation. What is the size of raindrops? What is the difference between light, moderate, and heavy drizzle? How do light, moderate, and heavy rain compare? For information, see Jack Williams, *The Weather Book* (New York: Vintage Books, 1992), p. 73.

4. *Rime* is ice formed when tiny drops of water rapidly freeze on contact with a surface. Hexagonal-shaped snowflakes form as water vapor *sublimes* (changes from a gas to a solid) on the surface of crystals. Are there any snowflakes that are alike? What is graupel? How do hailstones form? How do atmospheric conditions affect the formation of frozen precipitation? For information, see *The Weather Book,* pp. 95–105.

APPENDIX 1
Sources of Scientific Supplies

Catalog Suppliers

Carolina Biological Supply
   Company
2700 York Road
Burlington, NC 27215
(800) 334-5551

Connecticut Valley Biological
   Company
82 Valley Road
P.O. Box 326
Southampton, MA 01073
(800) 628-7748

Cuisenaire
10 Bank Street
P.O. Box 5026
White Plains, NY 10606
(800) 237-3142

Delta Education, Inc.
P.O. Box 915
Hudson, NH 03051-0915
(800) 258-1302

Fisher Scientific
Educational Materials Division
485 South Frontage Road
Burr Ridge, IL 60521
(708) 655-4410
(800) 766-7000

Frey Scientific Division of
   Beckley Cardy
100 Paragon Parkway
Mansfield, OH 44903
(800) 225-3739

NASCO
901 Janesville Avenue
P.O. Box 901
Fort Atkinson, WI 53538
(800) 677-2960

WWR/Sargent-Welch
911 Commerce Court
Buffalo Grove, IL 60089
(800) 727-4368

Ward's Natural Science
5100 West Henrietta Road
Rochester, NY 14586
(800) 962-2660

Sources of Rocks and Minerals

The following stores carry rocks
and minerals and are located in
many areas. To find the stores
near you, call the home offices:

Mineral of the Month Club
1290 Ellis Avenue
Cambria, CA 93428
(800) 941-5594

cambriaman@thegrid.net
www.mineralofthemonthclub.
   com

Nature Company
750 Hearst Avenue
Berkeley, CA 94701
(800) 227-1114

Nature of Things
10700 West Venture Drive
Franklin, WI 53132-2804
(800) 283-2921

The Discovery Store
15046 Beltway Drive
Dallas, TX 75244
(214) 490-8299

World of Science
900 Jefferson Road
Building 4
Rochester, NY 14623
(716) 475-0100

APPENDIX 2
Temperature Conversion Formulas

Convert Celsius to Fahrenheit

Example: Convert 100 degrees Celsius to Fahrenheit.

$$F = (1.8) \times {}^\circ C + 32$$
$$= (1.8) \times 100 + 32$$
$$= 180 + 32$$
$$= 212{}^\circ F$$

Convert Fahrenheit to Celsius

Example: Convert 212 degrees Fahrenheit to Celsius.

$${}^\circ C = \frac{{}^\circ F - 32}{1.8}$$
$$= \frac{212 - 32}{1.8}$$
$$= 100{}^\circ C$$

Convert Celsius to Kelvin

Example: Convert 30 degrees Celsius to Kelvin.

$$K = {}^\circ C + 273$$
$$= 30 + 273$$
$$= 303 \ K$$

Convert Kelvin to Celsius

Example: Convert 303 degrees Kelvin to Celsius.

$${}^\circ C = K - 273$$
$$= 303 - 273$$
$$= 30{}^\circ C$$

Astronomer's Flashlight

Materials

ruler
scissors
red transparent report folder

flashlight
rubber band

Procedure

1. Cut a 4 × 8-inch (10 × 20-cm) strip from the red folder.
2. Fold the strip in half to form a 4-inch (10-cm) square.
3. Cover the end of the flashlight with the square and secure with the rubber band.
4. Use the flashlight to read star maps outdoors at night.

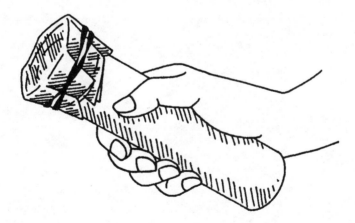

Results

An astronomer's flashlight is constructed.

Why?

When you move from a lighted area to a dark area, at first you can hardly see. After a few minutes, changes occur in your eyes and you see better. In about 30 minutes to 1 hour, the changes are complete and your vision is even better. Although your vision is not as good as in the light, it is the best it will be in the dark. You now have night vision.

One flash of white light can reverse the changes in the eye, causing you to lose your night vision. It takes another 30 to 60 minutes to get it back again. Red light affects night vision less than does white light, so the astronomer's flashlight is covered with a red filter. You can read your star map with the red light and still see the stars in the sky.

Glossary

absolute difference   Positive difference calculated by subtracting a smaller number from a larger number.

adhesive force   Attraction between like molecules.

air mass   Large body of air with about the same temperature and humidity throughout.

anticline   Fold producing an upward arch shape.

aquifer   Layer of permeable rock or regolith saturated with water and through which groundwater moves.

arc   Part of a circle.

arc length   Length of a portion of the circumference of a circle.

artesian well   Well in which groundwater from an aquifer rises naturally.

asthenosphere   Semiliquid layer below the lithosphere.

astrolabe   Instrument used to measure the altitude of a celestial object.

atmosphere   Gaseous envelope surrounding the Earth.

atmospheric pressure   Force that air exerts on a particular area. Also called air pressure.

atom   Smallest building block of nature; smallest particle of an element that retains the properties of that element; made up of protons, electrons, and neutrons.

axis   1. Straight line that passes through an object and around which the object turns. Earth's axis is an imaginary line that passes through the North and South Poles. 2. Line about which a three-dimensional structure is symmetrical.

axis orientation   Directional position of the axis of an object.

barometer   Instrument used to measure atmospheric pressure.

basal cleavage   Cleavage in one direction.

baseline   A straight line between two points from which an object is observed.

breccia   Clastic rocks that contain angular, rough-edged clasts with diameters of 0.08 inch (0.2 cm) or larger.

capillary attraction   Attractive force between a liquid and a solid causing liquid to be drawn into small tubelike openings.

celestial body   Natural object in the sky, such as a star, sun, moon, or planet.

celestial sphere   Imaginary sphere surrounding Earth on which appear stars and other celestial bodies.

cemented   Stuck together.

chemical bond   Attraction between atoms that holds them together in molecules.

chemical change   Change that produces one or more kinds of matter that are different from those present before the change; affects the chemical properties of a substance.

chemical composition   Elements and compounds that are present in a material.

chemical sedimentary rock   Rock formed when precipitates of minerals come out of solution and crystallize. Most of these chemical rocks are formed by evaporation of water from a solution and are called evaporites.

chemical weathering   Breakdown of crustal materials due to chemical changes of the substances making up the crust.

circumpolar star   Star that never sinks below the horizon of the observer but appears to revolve around a point in the sky above the Earth's axis.

clast   Loose rock fragment made up of bits of older rocks.

clastic rock   Sedimentary rock formed from clasts.

cleavage   Property of a mineral when it breaks along a cleavage plane.

cleavage plane   Flat surface along which a mineral breaks.

climate   Average weather in an area over a long period of time.

cloud   Visible atmospheric mass consisting of a high concentration of minute water droplets or ice crystals mixed in air.

cloud drop   Drop of water in a cloud with a diameter of 0.00004 to 0.002 inch (0.0001 to 0.005 cm).

coalescence   Union, as the merging of water drops that collide.

coarse-grained   Having large hard particles.

cohesive force   Attraction between unlike molecules.

cold front   Weather boundary where a cold air mass advances into a region occupied by a warm air mass; produces strong winds and rain.

compacted   Packed together.

compound   Matter made up of molecules that are all alike.

compression   Type of stress in the earth's crust where rocks are squeezed together.

concentrated   Gathered together in one place.

concentration Amount of substance dissolved or mixed in a specified quantity of a solution or mixture.

conchoidal A type of fracture with a shell-like surface.

condensate Liquid formed as a result of condensation.

condensation Phase change requiring a loss of energy in which a gas changes to a liquid.

condensation nuclei Small particles that attract water and encourage condensation.

conduction Transfer of heat by direct contact between materials.

conglomerate Clastic rocks that contain smooth, round-edged clasts with diameters of 0.08 inch (0.2 cm) or larger.

constructive interference Matching of crests and troughs of colliding waves.

continental air mass Air mass that forms over land.

contour interval Difference in elevation between one contour line and the next.

contour line Line on a topographic map that connects points of the same elevation.

convection Transfer of heat by the movement of heated fluids.

convection cell Pattern of air circulation caused by unequal heating of the Earth's surface.

convection current Up and down movement of air due to differences in temperature.

convergent boundary Place where two plates collide. Usually one plate moves under the other.

convert To change.

core Innermost layer of the Earth.

Coriolis effect Deflection of fluids as a result of the Earth's rotation.

covalent bond A strong attraction between two atoms that share an electron.

crest High point of a wave.

crust Outer layer of the Earth.

crystal Solid made up of atoms arranged in an orderly, regular pattern and forming flat faces.

crystal system Group of crystals based on their shape. The six common crystal systems are cubic, tetragonal, hexagonal, orthorhombic, monoclinic, and triclinic.

declination Location of a star in degrees north and south of the
celestial equator.

deferent In Ptolemy's model, the large circle around the Earth
along which the center of a planet's epicycle moved.

deflect To turn aside from a straight path.

dense Compact; crowded together.

density Comparison of the heaviness of a specific amount of a
material; mass of a substance per unit volume; measurement of
how much matter is packed into a certain volume.

deposition Buildup of sediments.

destructive interference Lack of matching of crests and troughs
of colliding waves.

dew point Temperature at which water vapor condenses.

dip Angle in degrees of the fault plane with a horizontal plane,
measured down from horizontal.

displaced Pushed out of the way.

divergent boundary A place where two plates move away from
each other.

downdraft Sinking air.

drizzle Precipitation in the liquid state; small droplets of water
that fall very close together and slowly as compared to rain.

Eastern Hemisphere Eastern half of the Earth, divided by longitude lines 0° and 180°. The longitude lines in this hemisphere are
labeled with an E, such as 45° E.

echo sounding Method of sending out sound from a sound transmitter and measuring its echo time.

echo time Time it takes sound leaving a transmitter to travel to an
object, be reflected, and return to a receiver.

electron Negatively charged subatomic particle.

element Matter made up of atoms that are alike.

elevation Height above sea level.

epicycle Small circle followed by a planet in Ptolemy's model of the
solar system. The center of the epicycle follows a larger circle
(deferent) around the Earth.

equator Imaginary line running east and west around the middle
of the Earth, equidistant to the Poles and located at 0° latitude.

erosion Process that includes weathering and the movement of
weathered material by natural forces from one place to another.

evaporation Phase change requiring a gain of energy in which a
liquid changes to a gas.

evaporite   Chemical sedimentary rock formed by the evaporation of water from a solution.

extrusive igneous rock   Fine-grained igneous rock formed at the Earth's surface.

face   Side of a crystal.

fathom   Length measurement equal to 6 feet (1.8 m).

fault   Fracture in the Earth's crust along which there is movement.

fault block   Block of rock that bounds a fault plane.

fault plane   Fracture line of a fault.

fault zone   Area of the Earth's crust that includes the fault blocks on both sides of the fault plane.

fine-grained   Having very small hard particles.

fluid   Gas or liquid.

folding   Bending of rock layers due to compressional stress.

foliated metamorphic rock   Striped-looking metamorphic rock with grains arranged in parallel bands.

footwall   Block of rock below a fault plane.

force   Push or pull exerted on matter; weight.

Foucault pendulum   Pendulum that shows the rotation of the Earth.

fracture   Property of a mineral when it doesn't break along a cleavage plane; an irregular break.

front   Boundary where two different air masses meet.

geocentric   Earth-centered.

graben   Down-dropped fault block bounded by parallel normal faults. Also called a rift. The rift valley formed by the displaced block is also called a graben.

grain   Hard particle.

gravity   Force that pulls celestial bodies toward each other; force that pulls everything on Earth toward the center of the Earth.

great circle   Circle on a sphere, with the center of the circle and the center of the sphere being the same.

greenhouse effect   Warming of the Earth by the trapping of infrared rays from the sun, just as the glass or plastic of a greenhouse traps infrared rays within it.

Greenwich Mean Time (GMT)   The standard time at the prime meridian.

groundwater   Water, such as from rainfall, that sinks into the ground.

hachure One of a set of short lines drawn inside a contour line to indicate a depression or crater. These lines always point downslope.

hackly A type of fracture with a jagged surface.

hanging wall Rock block above a fault plane.

hardness Measure of how difficult it is to scratch a mineral.

heft Subjective measurement of how heavy an object is. Heft is determined by picking up objects of equal volume and comparing their weights.

heliocentric Sun-centered.

hemisphere Half a sphere.

horizon Line where the sky appears to meet the Earth.

horse latitudes Regions between latitudes 23½° N and 23½° S. Also called tropics.

horst Upthrust fault block bounded by parallel normal faults.

humidity Amount of water vapor that is contained in air.

humus Brown or black soil material formed by decayed plants and animals.

hydrologic cycle Continuous interchange of water between the ocean, the land, plants, and clouds. Also called water cycle.

hydrosphere Total water on Earth.

hygrometer Instrument used to measure humidity.

hygroscopic Absorbing or attracting water from the air.

igneous rock Rock produced by the cooling and solidifying of liquid rock.

impermeable Not permitting passage, as of fluids, through its substance.

inertia Tendency of an object to remain stationary or to continue moving in a straight line unless acted on by an outside force.

infrared ray Invisible form of radiant energy that has a heating effect.

inner core Solid center of the Earth.

inorganic Not made from living things.

intrusive igneous rock Coarse-grained igneous rock formed underground.

inversion Layer of warm air lying above a layer of cold air in the atmosphere.

joint Fracture in strata along which there is no movement.

lateral fault Mainly horizontal movement of crust along the fault plane, to left or right, with little or no up or down movement. Also called a strike-slip fault.

latitude Distance in degrees north or south of the equator, which is located at 0° latitude.

lava Molten rock from within the Earth that reaches the Earth's surface.

left lateral fault Horizontal movement of fault blocks in which, to an observer looking directly at the fault, the motion of the block on the opposite side of the fault is to the left.

line of latitude Parallel.

line of longitude Meridian.

lithification Processes, including compaction and cementation, whereby newly deposited sediment is converted into sedimentary rock.

lithosphere Solid part of the Earth as compared with the gaseous and water parts (the atmosphere and the hydrosphere, respectively). Also specifically refers to the Earth's crust and upper mantle to a depth of about 60 miles (96 km).

longitude Distance east or west on the Earth's surface, measured in degrees from the prime meridian, which passes through Greenwich, England.

luster The way a mineral reflects light.

magma Molten rock beneath the Earth's surface.

magnetic field Region in which magnetic materials are acted on by magnetic forces.

mantle Layer surrounding the Earth's core. Its thickness is about 1,812 miles (2,900 km).

maritime air mass Air mass that forms over an ocean.

mass Amount of material in a substance.

matter Any substance that has mass and occupies space; made up of tiny particles called atoms.

mean solar day Average length of the solar days over a year; 24 hours.

mechanical weathering Breakdown of crustal materials by physical means.

medium-grained Having particles that are a size between coarse- and fine-grained.

meridian   Line of longitude. Each meridian is a whole or a half of a great circle, imaginary lines on the Earth's surface passing through the Earth's North and South Poles on a globe.

mesosphere   Solid layer of the mantle below the mantle's asthenosphere layer.

metamorphic rock   Rock that has been changed by great heat and pressure within the Earth's crust.

metamorphism   Change in structure, appearance, and composition of rock in the solid state within the Earth's crust as a result of changes in temperature and pressure.

midocean ridge   One of a number of ridges forming a continuous chain of underwater mountains around the Earth.

mineral   Single, solid element or compound found in the Earth. It has four basic characteristics: (1) it occurs naturally; (2) it is inorganic; (3) it has a definite chemical composition; and (4) it has a crystalline structure.

molecule   Combination of two or more atoms.

neutron   Neutrally charged subatomic particle.

noon   Time at which the sun crosses the local meridian and is at its highest point above the Earth's horizon; twelve o'clock in the daytime.

normal fault   Fault in which the hanging wall moves down in relation to the footwall.

North Pole   Northernmost point on the Earth.

Northern Hemisphere   Region of the Earth north of the equator.

occluded front   Boundary where a cold air mass meets a cool air mass under a warm air mass.

orbit   Curved path that a satellite traces around a celestial body.

outer core   Liquid layer below the mesosphere and above the solid inner core.

oxidation   Combination with oxygen.

parallax   Apparent change in the position of an object when viewed from different locations.

parallax angle (p)   One-half of the apparent change in a star's angular position.

parallax distance   Linear distance between the apparent positions of an object due to parallax.

parallel   Line of latitude. The parallels are imaginary circles around a globe that run parallel to each other and perpendicular to the meridians, imaginary lines on the Earth's surface.

pendulum Suspended object that swings back and forth.

percolation Passing or seeping of groundwater or any liquid through a permeable material.

permeability Measure of how easily a solid allows fluids to pass through it.

permeable Material that is capable of having substances, such as fluids, move through its pore spaces.

phase Shape of the moon as seen from the Earth; one of the forms in which matter may be found: solid, liquid, or gas.

phase composition Phase of matter that is present.

physical change Change in which the appearance of matter changes but its properties and makeup remain the same.

pi Math value equaling 3.14.

planar projection Circular map that shows only one hemisphere of the Earth.

plate Section of the lithosphere.

plate tectonics Theory that the Earth's lithosphere is divided into sections called plates. These plates float on top of the asthenosphere, much like flat rocks on thick mud.

polar air mass Air mass that forms near the Poles.

polar circumference Distance around the Earth from Pole to Pole.

Polaris North Star; star above the Earth's north geographic pole.

pollutant Substances that destroy the purity of air, water, or land.

pore space Small, narrow spaces between particles in materials, such as soil, sand, or rocks.

porosity Percentage of a material's volume that is pore space.

porphyritic rock Intrusive igneous rock containing two or more different sizes of interlocking crystals; thus is said to have varied grain sizes.

precipitate To separate in solid form from a solution.

precipitation All forms of water that fall from the atmosphere.

prime meridian Meridian running through Greenwich, England, located at 0° longitude.

proportion Statement of equality between two ratios.

proton Positively charged subatomic particle.

psychrometer Hygrometer used to measure relative humidity.

radiant energy Energy that can travel through space in the form of waves, including gamma rays, X rays, ultraviolet rays, infrared rays, radio waves, and visible light.

radiation Transfer of heat by emission of heat waves.

ratio Comparison of one value to anther; written as a fraction.

recrystallization Enlargement of minerals.

regional metamorphism Metamorphism that occurs when large areas of rock are changed by pressure and heat, such as mountain building.

regolith Loose, uncemented, weathered rock, including soil, that covers the Earth's surface.

relative humidity Ratio between the amount of water vapor present in the air and the amount of water vapor the air can hold at that temperature; expressed as a percentage.

reradiate To emit previously absorbed radiation.

reverse fault Fault in which the hanging wall moves upward in relation to the footwall.

revolve To move in a curved path around an object.

rift See **graben**.

rift valley Long, narrow break in the Earth's crust.

right lateral fault Horizontal movement of fault blocks in which, to an observer looking directly at the fault, the motion of the block on the opposite side of the fault is to the right.

rime Ice layer formed when tiny drops of water rapidly freeze on contact with a surface.

rock Solid cohesive mixture of one or more minerals.

rock cycle Changing of rocks from one type to another by a series of processes involving heat, pressure, melting, cooling, and sedimentation.

rotate To turn about an axis.

runoff Rainwater that is unable to soak into the ground and moves over its surface.

satellite Celestial body that revolves about another celestial body.

saturated Soaked thoroughly so that all pore space is filled.

saturated solution Solution in which the solvent has dissolved the maximum amount of solute at a given temperature.

scientific method Technique of finding answers through determining a purpose and a hypothesis, undertaking research and experimentation, and determining a conclusion.

seafloor spreading Process of the creation of new oceanic crust that moves slowly away from the midocean ridges.

sediment Regolith that has been transported by agents of erosion and deposited in another place.

sedimentary rock Rock formed by deposits of sediment.

settling rate Time it takes sediment to settle out of its transporting agent.

shear Stress that twists, tears, or pushes rocks past one another.

sidereal day Time it takes for a celestial body to make one complete rotation on its axis.

silicate Common compound found in the rocky material in the Earth's crust.

slope Measure of the steepness of an inclined surface.

soil Top layer of regolith that supports plant growth. It is composed of particles from rock mixed with humus.

solar day Interval of time required for a meridian to pass by the sun (at noon) twice.

solar system A group of celestial bodies including nine planets, moons, asteroids, and comets revolving around a star—our Sun.

solute Substance in a solution that is dissolved.

solution Mixture of two or more substances whose makeup is the same throughout.

solvent Substance in a solution that dissolves another substance.

sonar Term standing for *SO*und *N*avigation *A*nd *R*anging.

sounding Early method of measuring depth with a weighted line marked with distance measurements.

source region Region where an air mass forms; maritime, polar, continental, and tropical.

South Pole Southernmost point on the Earth.

Southern Hemisphere Region of the Earth south of the equator.

specific gravity (sp. gr.) Ratio of the mass of a mineral in air to the mass of the water displaced by the mineral.

splintery A type of fracture producing surfaces that are small, thin, and sharp.

standard time Time within time zones; based on the time of a mean solar day of 24 hours; clock time.

stationary front Boundary between warm and cold air masses that does not move.

stellar parallax Parallax angle of a star.

strata (pl. of **stratum**)   Layers of rock material in the Earth's crust.

streak   Color of the powder left when a mineral is rubbed against a rough surface that is harder than the mineral.

streak plate   Surface of unglazed porcelain or other material against which a mineral is rubbed in a common streak test.

stress   Force that acts on rocks in the Earth's crust, causing movement or a change in shape or volume.

strike-slip fault   See **lateral fault**.

sublime   To change from a gas to a solid.

superposition   The placement of one wave atop another when they meet.

suspension   A mixture made of parts that separate upon standing. Formed when water mixes with substances that do not dissolve.

syncline   Downfold creating a troughlike shape.

synodic month   Time required for the Moon's phases to complete one cycle from one new moon to the next: 29½ days.

tension   Type of stress resulting in the stretching, or pulling apart, of rocks.

texture   Size of grains in materials such as rock, sand, or soil.

thermal metamorphism   Metamorphism due to heat.

three-dimensional   Having three measurements: height, width, and length.

time meridian   Central meridian in a time zone; the meridians every 15° east and west of the prime meridian.

time zone   One of 24 divisions on Earth, each 15° longitude wide (with slight variations for practical purposes) and differing from each other by 1 hour. All locations within a time zone keep the same standard time.

topographic map   Flat map that shows the shapes and heights of land areas using lines that connect points on the Earth that have the same elevation.

topography   The description of the size, shape, and elevation of a region of land.

transform boundary   Place where two plates slide horizontally in opposite directions alongside each other.

transpiration   Loss of water by evaporation through the surface of plant leaves.

tropic   Either of the two regions north and south of the equator to latitudes 23½° N and 23½° S. The tropics are also called horse latitudes.

tropical air mass Air mass that forms over the tropics.

troposphere Layer of the atmosphere next to the Earth.

trough Low point of a wave.

updraft Rising air.

van der Waals bond A weak electrostatic attraction between atoms that is easily broken.

warm front Weather boundary where a warm air mass advances into a region occupied by a cold air mass; produces cloudy skies, rain, or snow.

water table Boundary line between the zone of aeration and the zone of saturation.

water vapor Water in the gas phase.

wave Disturbance in a material, such as the surface of water, that repeats itself.

wave height Vertical, or top-to-bottom, distance between the crest and the trough of a wave.

wavelength Horizontal distance between similar points on two successive waves.

weather Condition of the atmosphere in a specific place at a particular time, such as pressure, temperature, humidity, winds, precipitation, and clouds.

weathering Process by which rocks are broken into smaller pieces.

well Shaft sunk into the water table.

Western Hemisphere Western half of the Earth, divided by longitude lines 0° and 180°. The longitude lines in this hemisphere are labeled with a W, such as 45° W.

wind Movement of air in a general horizontal direction.

zenith Point of highest altitude in the sky for a celestial body.

zone of aeration Underground layer starting at the surface in which the pore spaces of rocks and soil are filled with air.

zone of saturation Underground layer starting directly below the zone of aeration, in which the pore spaces of rocks and soil are filled with water.

Index

breccia
    definition of, 43–45
    model of, 105

capillary attraction
    definition of, 152, 211
    demonstration of, 152
celestial body
    definition of, 11, 211
celestial sphere, 50, 212
chemical bonds
    definition of, 70, 212
    model of, 70–71
chemical change, 99, 212
chemical composition, 74, 212
chemical sedimentary rock
    definition of, 105, 212
    evaporites, 106, 215
    formation of, 105–106
chemical weathering, 99, 212
circumpolar star
    definition of, 47, 212
    model of, 47–49
clast
    definition of, 105, 212
    lithification of, 105
clastic rock
    breccia, 105
    classes of, 106
    conglomerate, 105, 213
    formation of, 105
clay, 113
cleavage
    basal, 84, 211
    definition of, 84, 212
    mica, 84
    plane, 84, 212
    types of, 84
cleavage plane, 84, 212
climate
    definition of, 165, 212
cloud
    definition of, 184, 212
    drops, 201, 202
    formation of, 184
    seeding of, 202–203
    types of, 184
cloud drops
    coalescence, 202, 212
    definition of, 201, 212

    growth of, 202
    size of, 201
coalescence
    of cloud drops, 202
    definition of, 202, 212
coarse-grained, 92, 212
cohesive force, 154, 212
compound, 70, 212
compression, 116, 212
concentrated, 165, 212
concentration, 184, 212
conchoidal, 84, 213
condensate
    definition of, 184
    formation of, 184
condensation, 156, 213
condensation nuclei
    definition of, 201, 213
    water drop formation, 201
conduction
    definition of, 170, 213
conglomerate, 105, 213
constructive interference, 147, 213
continental air mass, 183, 213
contour intervals, 17, 213
contour lines
    definition of, 17, 213
    model of, 17–18
convection
    definition of, 171, 213
    experiment, 175–179
convection cell
    definition of, 178, 213
    downdrafts, 178, 179–214
    model of, 178–179
    updrafts, 178, 179, 223
convection currents
    definition of, 175, 213
    experiment 175–177
convergent boundary
    definition of, 132, 213
    model of, 132
Copernicus, Nicolaus, 36
core
    chemical composition of, 74
    definition of, 74, 213
    models of, 73–76
Coriolis effect
    definition of, 28, 213
    model of, 28–29